Awaken the Genius

Good better best, never rest
Till good be better, and better best

Your child's achieving attitude begins with you.

If your child senses your strong support and belief that he has 'that' extra special quality in him, he will rise to it naturally.

Teaching your child is important. Teaching your child to think is more important. Thinking is not information or knowledge or being right. Thinking is the skill which unlocks the potential within and determines how intelligence and information are to be used. This is the essential difference that separates winners and achievers from others.

Using day-to-day experiences and examples, this book shows how, with parental guidance, and supported with practical exercises and activities, your child can become an achiever. Written in a simple, lucid style, this book is almost an across-the-table conversation with a caring parent.

Remember, geniuses are not born. They are nurtured.

Nurture your child. Accept the challenge!

The Author

Born in a well-known family of Brahmin priests in Bangalore, Shakuntala Devi received her early lessons in mathematics from her grandfather. By the age of five, she was recognised as a child prodigy and an expert in complex mental arithmetic. A year later she demonstrated her talents to a large assembly of students and professors at the University of Mysore.

Hailed as an authentic heroine of our times her feats are recorded in the *Guiness Book of World Records.* She made international headlines for out-performing and out-computing the most sophisticated computers in the world.

Yet Shakuntala Devi disliked being called the 'human computer'. She strongly believed that people have minds better than any computer. Her passionate interest in exploring and expanding the learning capacity of the human mind led her to develop the concept of 'mind dynamics'.

She maintains that a child's curiosity and receptivity during infancy and childhood can never be matched, and we must, as parents, nurture the young minds by offering the right learning process and motivation to develop the innate strengths possessed by every child.

This book is a result of her cumulative experience in mind dynamics.

AWAKEN the GENIUS in YOUR CHILD

Shakuntala Devi
Illustrated by Pulak Biswas

Orient
Paperbacks
DELHI | MUMBAI

ISBN : 978-81-222-0189-5

Awaken the Genius in Your Child

Subject: Family & Relationships / Parenting

© Shakuntala Devi

1st Published 1998
23rd Printing 2020

Published by
Orient Paperbacks
(A division of Vision Books Pvt. Ltd.)
5A/8 Ansari Road, New Delhi-110 002
www.orientpaperbacks.com

Cover design by Vision Studio
Cover Image © Imagebazaar.com
Illustrated by Pulak Biswas

Printed and bound at Thomson Press (I) Ltd.

CONTENTS

1

Your Child: A Gift from God

Every child comes with the message that God is not yet tired of Man.

Rabindranath Tagore

Did you know that you have the power to turn your child into a genius? Yes, you have! Hold on to that dynamic thought. Let it seep into you. Make it a part of your mental process. And it will never let you or your child down because of one simple fact. It is the truth.

In all great religions and philosophies of the world, a child is considered a gift from God. Have you ever stopped to consider why? It is because every child is a marvel of creation. That is obvious from the day the infant is born. It moves its tiny limbs; it cries. How does the infant do all that and more?

The Brain — The Seat of Genius

Think. Within the child is a miracle — a powerful force; an awe-inspiring phenomenon provided by nature, a great gift that links the child to the external world — the brain! The brain that is least understood, but used most often — a bottomless well from which the child can draw on the refreshing waters to quench his eternal thirst for knowledge; a seat from which he can discover the

7

myriad ways that are available to him to fulfill his dreams, visions and aspirations.

He can do all that provided you are there to guide him; to help develop this inexhaustible reservoir; to help him explore its tremendous potential. You can help the child if you believe you can do it. It is your confidence that will be transmitted to the child from a very young age. With your support and your inputs, the child will never suffer from a feeling of inadequacy or inferiority that can be barriers to success. Instead, the youngster will develop a spirit of confidence that will assist in releasing those inner powers, that all-important untapped potential — the genius within.

Look up any encyclopaedia. You will find listed there the seven ancient wonders of the world — the Sphinx in Egypt; the Hanging Gardens of Babylon; the Great Wall of China; the Taj Mahal of India; the Catacombs in Rome; the Leaning Tower of Pisa; the Collosus of Rhodes.... But how did all these great wonders come into being? What was the inspirational source of these structures?

Look within yourself for the answer — the brain. That magnificent, one-and-a-half kilogram mushroom, composed of grey and white tissue, which contains something like 30 billion neurons and, at least, 150 billion glial cells — your child is born with it! What a marvellous God-given gift it is! It has thoughts that, if released, could glut all the telephone exchanges in the world put together! It could defeat the most sophisticated computer ever invented.

The most exciting news is that your child has it. Your child possesses this great generator. But of what use is a generator if the power is not released? The controls are in your hands.

Create a Healthy Atmosphere

As a good parent, you provide shelter for your child; you clothe your child; you feed your child with good, healthy, nourishing food. In the same way, it is imperative that you provide a good atmosphere with excellent facilities, and feed your child's brain with wholesome, healthy, nourishing, educative thoughts. For these are the very foundation of a genius.

Your child's brain is fresh and unpolluted. It is like an unending plot of land with acres and acres of rich, fertile soil. If neglected, it will grow wild and untamed. But if you plant the seeds of education carefully, tend them tirelessly and nurture them endlessly, you will harvest a crop that will be invaluable — you will nurture a genius!

Fill your child's mind with ever-fresh, ever-new creative thoughts. It is the greatest, the best grounding you can give your child. After all, when Ralph Waldo Emerson, one of the greatest thinkers of our times, said: 'A man is what he thinks about all day long', he was referring to every human being. By instilling healthy, educative thoughts into your child, the latter will lead a healthy, educated life. The shrubs that you nurture within the child will grow steadily into a tall, strong tree. And he or she will tower over the world like a Collosus.

There are innumerable examples of children who have performed wonders and been proclaimed geniuses. There was the child who could recite long Sanskrit verses from the Vedas at the drop of a hat. Another would push aside his set of playing blocks, and talk to you about Angkor Vat, a temple in Kampuchea. He would tell you that it was built by King Suryavarman II in dedication to Lord Vishnu. Yet another child would speak a foreign language fluently. Still another would glance at a long column of numbers and give you the total even before you could pull out your calculator!

Is every such child a genius? Yes. But even as we marvel at such a genius, we do not stop to think of the tremendous inputs that have gone into his or her fresh, tender mind. The atmosphere, the environment for awakening the genius in the child has been provided by parents who care — and most important — who believe.

Believe in Your Child

Contrast the above examples with a lady I met some years ago. She was a home maker, a good, loving mother. She encouraged her young 12-year-old daughter to study, to go on field-projects, to write poems and essays, to work out intricate mathematical problems. Yet, she complained, 'My daughter never does well at school. Her marks are average. What can I do?'

I listened thoughtfully to everything she said. Then I drew her aside, out of hearing distance of her daughter. I complimented her on her hard work. 'But,' I said, 'if you will forgive me, I'd like to point out one thing you are lacking in.'

'What is that?' she asked eagerly.

'Belief,' I replied simply. 'Belief in your daughter's abilities. You are making her do all those things. But you are also holding her back because you do not have confidence in her.'

'What should I do?' she asked humbly.

'Believe in her,' I said firmly. 'And you will communicate that sense of belief to your daughter. So far, she has obeyed you, done everything you've asked her to do without really understanding why — without enjoying it, without believing in it or herself.'

The woman went away saying, 'You have opened my eyes!'

There was nothing complex in my advice. It was the simple truth. Only if you believe that you can tap your child's genius, will you be able to do it. Only if you believe in your child, will you be able to kindle the best in the youngster. The child is already endowed with mental faculties by nature. Within the brain there is already an exalted intellectual power. The child is already extraordinarily imaginative; possesses a highly inventive capacity, is blessed with a colourful, creative mind. But it is your confidence, your inputs laced with large doses of belief, that will enable the child to exploit them to their fullest potential.

You can explain various subjects patiently and at length to your child. But at the end of it, if you lament over the child's

'mediocrity', you will undo all the good you have, so carefully, worked upon. You will instil into your child's brain that he or she is not bright. And at the end of it, the child will bring you an average report card which will be the direct outcome of your negative attitude. Only by constantly expressing confidence in your child, will you elicit the best results from him or her.

The most obvious example of a parent's belief transplanting itself successfully into a child is that of Jawaharlal Nehru and Indira Gandhi. Nehru believed in his daughter. He believed that one day she would become the Prime Minister of India. In turn, she believed in it herself. The rest, of course, is history!

Of course, there are many examples that may not fit in with what I have just written. When she was a young girl, Madame Schumann-Heink was rejected by her singing teacher. The young aspirant was advised to return to her sewing machine. The implication was obvious. The child, according to the teacher, was no nightingale. She possessed no talent for singing. She was best suited to be a seamstress. But the young girl's belief in herself overshadowed the lack of confidence her singing teacher had in her, and, finally, won the day. She rose to be one of the all-time

greats in opera-singing. How hard it must have been for her to struggle through that rejection!

Not every person would have had her strength of conviction. By disbelieving a child's ability, you could be subverting a genius. On the other hand, if you radiate a strong belief in your child's genius, you will provide the warmth and sunshine necessary for a bud to blossom into a flower. If you believe in your child, your child will achieve!

To Conclude

All parents want their child to be a genius. However, your child's attainments begin with you.

- Believe that you can make your child a genius.
- Believe in your child's ability to become a genius.
- Never show by word or gesture, that you feel your child is 'mediocre'.

2

Give Your Child an Early Start

If you can give your son only one gift, let it be enthusiasm.

Bruce Barton

Wouldn't you like to be one of those proud parents who exclaims in wonder, 'My one-year-old can read!' Of course, you would. And you can make it come true. But before I go on to the method, I think it is extremely important to raise one critical question in your mind. A question that you, as a responsible parent, ought to ask yourself. It may require some honest soul-searching. But it would be worth it. The question is: 'Why?' Ask yourself again and again, 'Why do I want my one-year-old child to read? Why do I want my child to be a genius?'

I cannot stress enough, the absolute importance — the imperativeness of this question. Your motive should be of great concern to you because it is going to have an effect on your child.

Let us start with the obvious. You want your child to be a genius because you want the best for him or her. You want your child to be a success. A commendable goal! But apart from being an achiever, you also want your child to be a free, happy, fulfilled person — a creative individual, who enjoys what he or she is doing.

14

Once you have that clear in your mind, you are ready to go on to take that first step. But at every step, remember one positive principle: *I want the best for my child, so I must give my best to my child.* Keep that in mind. Repeat it to yourself as often as you can. Make it a part of your daily food for thought. This way, you will consciously create an exciting, energising atmosphere. Your positive thought-pattern will nurture your child's intelligence. And in this lush, life-giving, creative atmosphere, your child's genius will bloom and flourish.

Why does the exotic tulip grow only in the fields of the Netherlands? Because Holland provides this exotic flora with the right soil, the right temperature and the right moisture for it to flourish. Similarly, your child's genius — an exotic, God-given gift — will flower in conducive conditions created by you.

Guide Gently; Don't Order

A child is very sensitive to the tone you use. Modulate your voice so that you sound gentle. Unnecessarily upsetting the child will never elicit the results you desire. Learning should be an enjoyable experience for the child. But it won't be if the youngster feels he is being imposed upon.

Have Reasonable Expectations

Child psychologists have found that upto the age of about six years, a child's attention span does not exceed more than two minutes on one subject. For example, after two minutes, your daughter may lose interest in the activity she is engaged in and start playing with her doll. Popular educational serials such as *Sesame Street* have been made with this point in mind. So don't force her to come back on to your track. It will only irritate her. Have patience. If your expectations are too high, the child will be under undue stress.

Why are these two points so important? Parents, being human, are apt to be over-zealous and could over-extend themselves as well as the child. In your eagerness, even your anxiety to get on with nurturing a genius, you could forget one very important factor: the child's happiness. Here is where a studied restraint is required on your part. Let your instincts guide you to guide your child. The reason: for the child, his/her genius should be a blessing, never a burden.

Sir Julian Huxley wrote: 'We, Mankind, contain the possibilities of the earth's immense future, and can realise more and more of them on condition that we increase our knowledge and love.' Knowledge and love — that is what you should impart to your child.

The Information Age

We are living today in a world suitable for a genius — an ever-evolving, ever-changing kaleidoscope of high-tech in every space of life. Information and more information blinks at us from every corner of this world. The pace may appear frenetic to those weaned on old yardsticks. But for the child of today — the citizen of tomorrow — this feverish pace of development will appear to be normal, provided you start him out early in his quest for knowledge. Knowledge will help your child to understand the new world in relation to himself. With the passing of centuries, the world has evolved from the Ice Age to the Stone Age, the Bronze Age, and so on. In every era, Man has taken great changes and challenges in his stride, even using extremely challenging circumstances to better his life. He is now in the Information Age, where he is surrounded with a variety of media — newspapers, magazines, video, computers, and so on. These are but poor relations of the greatest, most intricate, most sophisticated means of information network that was ever created — the brain.

With reams of information zipping across vast oceans in the time it takes for you to read this sentence, it is no wonder that we feel that the world is shrinking. Simultaneously, the brain that receives, digests, stores, acts on and reacts to such information is expanding proportionately. Your child is, indeed, a citizen of the Information Age from the day he or she is born.

From the minute the infant heralds his entry into the world with a loud wail, the child steps into an environment that is going to test his abilities to the utmost. And if you, with your adult understanding, nurture his capabilities, he will find it as easy as eating cake.

Nurture a Love for Knowledge

Being a responsible parent, you will have to recognise and accept the fact that you and your child have entered a world of challenges

— a new age of education, where you must, effectively, *nurture* the child with modern, dynamic thoughts rather than follow the traditional approach to education. I will not pause to explain the above words since they are self-explanatory. To proceed, the *nurturist* parent can, indeed, turn the child into a genius with the right parental pre-training and guidance at home. You can increase and enhance the child's intelligence at a very early age — the earlier, the better.

Since new ideas are, very often, met with resistance, let me emphasise that in no way am I suggesting that you burden the child. As I have already explained in this chapter, it is your attitude that is going to affect the child's attitude. If you create the right atmosphere, adopt the *fun-to-learn* credo, your child will chortle his way to becoming a genius.

However, if you are a new-age parent, you may well ask, 'What will my child gain by learning to read by the time he or she is one year old?' Let me put it this way: Your child has everything to gain and nothing to lose. I will elaborate on this as I go on.

By introducing your child to reading at a very early age, you are passing a powerful current of knowledge through the young brain. And by doing so, you are opening the door to a greater world, which, under traditional circumstances, he would enter when he is about four or five years old. By doing this, you are giving him a headstart. And by this very stimulation, you are raising the child's visionary abilities (I mean this in the metaphorical sense) at an early age. The world, after all, does need visionaries.

The Fun-to-Learn Attitude

If you handle matters right by adhering to the principle — *I want the best for my child, so I must give my best to him/her;* if you adopt the *fun-to-learn* attitude, you are planting within the child's mind, a deep-seated yearning to learn at an early age. The child will

develop a thirst for greater knowledge that will always stand him in good stead.

The fun-to-learn attitude also has an important factor built into it. For example, I know a mother who used every opportunity possible to educate her child whether it was at the table over a meal, while playing with her blocks, watching a movie, having a bath.... It did not diminish her young daughter's enjoyment, and, instead, simultaneously increased her vocabulary and enhanced her spelling skills. What was the mother doing? She was inculcating in the child, a natural feeling that learning and studying are a part of life. The child in question grew up with this invaluable training ingrained in her mind. Today, she is eleven years old. To her, playing with her friends or doing her homework are equally enjoyable activities. I can guarantee that as this child grows older and is confronted with an excessively demanding study schedule, she will never suffer from pre-examination blues or have that miserable 'I-have-to-swot' feeling.

Starting Early Gives You a Choice

Finally, there is one more significant dimension to starting the child early. A child psychologist once told me: 'A greater intelligence gives the child choice.' It does. It provides the child with a bright shiny key to newer and more rewarding experiences at an early age. The genius can, by his extraordinary powers, influence events and control his own destiny.

I am reminded here of a passing acquaintance. During the course of my many travels, I met a millionaire who lived like a pauper. He had started life as a boy-waiter. He carried tea to and from the stock exchange. Being bright and inquisitive, he invested his measly earnings, comprising largely of tips, in shares. As his capital increased, he started dealing in real estate. Today he can have anything for the asking. But he does not live in a mansion. He still resides in a little cottage, dresses in simple clothes, does not have a battalion of servants, owns no Rolls Royce. He has experienced the good life and wallowed in luxuries, but, for some reason, has preferred to return to his original lifestyle. 'Why did you do that?' I asked him. 'Surely you don't have to prove anything to yourself or anybody else!'

'No,' he replied thoughtfully. 'I live like this out of choice.'

Choice — what a wonderful word! I would liken the highly developed intelligence of a child to this millionaire's wealth. A millionaire can choose to live in poverty. But the pauper cannot choose to live a lavish life of luxury. So it is with your child. By starting his education early, you are developing his special gifts and giving him the right to choose and control his own destiny. And you are doing this by nurturing his most valuable asset, a wealth greater than any money in the world can buy — his brain.

After you have read and digested this chapter, you will have realised that you should go on to the next one only if you are convinced about turning your child into a genius.

To Conclude

The making of a genius carries within it, a complex interaction between honest motivation, the right attitude and a far-sighted perception. From this intricate tapestry, emerges the dynamics of genius. It is a thought that is as potent and as inspiring, as it is humbling.

3

Sowing the Seeds of Genius

He who would climb the ladder must begin at the bottom.

Proverb

My baby pointed at an alphabet and said, "A"! And she was right! My God, can you believe it? And she's only two!'

'Really? That's wonderful! Did you teach her that?'

'No. She must be a born genius!'

I overheard this conversation between two young women when I was at the chemist recently. As they left, still talking excitedly, I mused over how easy it was to believe that a two-year-old toddler had been magically and mysteriously transformed into a *born genius*. Obviously, somebody in the family had taught the child. The mother, unknowingly, was attributing the child's ability to some higher mystical power. Would she be disappointed if she were to learn that it was, perhaps, her sister, who had coached the baby on one of her many visits, I wondered.

Sadly, it is this kind of an incidental happening that makes parents feel that their child must be a 'born' genius. Some parents, at such similar discoveries, take more interest and start nurturing the child's 'inborn' genius. Others remain breathless observers, only to be disappointed that their child's early promise didn't bear fruit later on in school. The problem is that *until every parent realises that every child's brain is a God-given gift, and that every child can be nurtured into a genius,* society will continue to applaud a few 'discoveries', while neglecting the majority. What a waste of invaluable wealth!

Catch them Young

You can strike gold if you take the right steps to turn your child into a genius, starting now! Here, I would like to narrate another interesting incident. Recently, I bumped into an old friend, who is a journalist. As we exchanged old memories, I suddenly recalled something and exclaimed, 'Do you remember the time when you were only three years old?'

'What about it?' she asked.

'You didn't know how to read. Yet, you could identify the first line of every song written on those old 78 rpm records!'

'Yes,' she said, a smile playing upon her lips.

'Your father would say, "Bring Que Sera Sera" or whatever. And you'd obediently trot off, sift through that stack of records, and always, unerringly, bring the right one!'

We were silent for a long time, remembering. Then, I asked her curiously, 'How did you do it?'

'I don't know,' she shrugged. 'Perhaps each record had a different-coloured label,' she guessed.

'No,' I said definitely. Having sifted through them myself, I knew that they had all been of one colour, one shade — red.

'It's still talked about at our family gatherings,' she grinned, 'like a great event!'

'It was,' I said quietly.

Now, don't get me wrong. My friend is very intelligent, an extremely gifted writer, perhaps, even an unproclaimed genius. But it only proves my point. She cannot remember how or why she could identify the records as a three-year-old. Looking back, however, I think I know how she did it. Her musical-minded mother had, unwittingly, taught her how to read and recognize the names of the records. She had imparted this reading ability without making any conscious effort to do so. At that time, my friend could barely read each alphabet, yet, she could identify the entire first line of every song!

While most people would look upon this as an exceptional ability, let me put it in perspective. It is a phenomenon only because it happens so rarely. But it can happen all the time if we work on it. You can make even your one-year-old read. How will you do that? Will it require some complicated procedure? Will it be difficult? Will it be a strain on the child? Before you close your mind to the suggestion, let me assure you that the technique requires little effort on your part. In fact, it is so simple that you will wonder why you had not thought of it yourself! It is called the Flashcard Technique.

But before you launch into it, make sure that your infant has been fed, burped and is generally comfortable with himself. If he is sleepy, there is no point in trying to keep him awake. If you are his parent, Nature is a higher parent. Perhaps you think I am sermonising. But in your enthusiasm, you could justifiably get carried away. And if the sleepy child's attention wanders or he becomes irritable, you could hardly be blamed for throwing up your hands and giving up!

Also, the atmosphere should be one of play, fun and games. Impart to your child, through your enthusiastic attitude (I'd even go as far as to say — your body language), that what you are about to do is fun — like going out. You have probably realised that the moment, 'going out' is mentioned, your child pricks up his ears, and by pointing his little finger towards the door, indicates in no uncertain terms where his interests lie! If your child's little antenna picks up the idea that he and you are about to indulge in a game akin to going out, you can be sure that he will be an eager participant, or rather, a playmate!

The Flashcard Technique

It would interest you to learn that the Flashcard Technique is used for children as well as adults! Language students are advised by their tutors to carry with them, a batch of cards with foreign words or phrases written down on one side. The other side contains the translation in their own mother tongue or the language they are proficient in. This technique serves as an excellent, and extremely useful and easy guide for students.

1. Cut large pieces of clean, white, blank paper into squares of about ten by ten inches. Paste them on similarly cut, thick cardboard pieces or stiffer paper.

2. On each piece of paper, write one simple word in large, bold, capital letters. Each piece of paper should, of course, bear a different word. Initially, use a word by which the child can identify the object. For example, on one, write CAT; on another, DOG; on yet another, CAR. Then, there are other words like: CHAIR, MOTHER, and so on.

3. Now show each card to your child and enunciate the word clearly. For example, as you show him CAT, say the word CAT.

4. Repeat the word over and over again, displaying the card and enunciating the word.

5. Increase the difficulty level gradually, going on to longer words as you realise that the child is catching on.

Keep adding new phrases to the collection of words, and discard what the children have become familiar with. Similarly, you can devise new cards with new words for your child, and throw away the older ones once you are convinced he will not need them any longer.

There is no fixed time element here. Your child could learn within days, weeks or even months. It will not be your child's ability at test here, but yours. Your attitude, your patience, your perseverance — these will be tried. You will have to evolve your own method to make the child feel that learning is a fun-experience.

To give you an illustration: Maya Rao, a kindergarten teacher, had her own method of teaching her daughter. She would hide the card behind her and approach the child playfully, saying, 'What does Mama have for her baby, Sneha?' One-year-old Sneha would look up expectantly. She would try and reach for the mysterious object. Then, Maya would, with a flourish, bring out the card and announce triumphantly — CAT! The child's answering chortle of delight proved that the technique was having the desired effect.

In no time at all, Sneha could read words. Soon, she graduated to phrases. Maya was unstinting in her efforts towards her daughter's education. She bought various simple books. Every book was like a treasure of knowledge for little Sneha. By the time she was four, the little girl surprised everybody by her familiarity with words and sentences.

Why was Maya's Flashcard Technique a success? Her belief in her child, a caring and positive attitude, infinite patience on her part — all made Sneha look forward to these sessions. And each one was equally exciting and rewarding for the child.

The Flashcard Technique uses the sight-reading method. As the child becomes familiar with shapes and lines, he may not know the alphabets individually, but he will recognize the word gradually. By introducing the child to new words, you can increase his vocabulary.

Familiarity with Sounds

You can go one more step forward. Gradually, you can teach him the sound of letters as this is closely linked with sight-reading.

You can take two flashcards beginning with the same letter and sound, for example — MOTHER and MILK. To that, you can add others — MUD, MAT, MAN, and so on.

Soon, you can compile cards with familiar words beginning with the combined sound of two alphabets, such as CH as in CHAIR and CHECK; SH as in SHAVE and SHARK; TH as in THING, THUMB, and so on.

Farozan Warsi, a mother of two little girls recalled how she had taught her children.

'SH is what I tell you when I want you to be quiet,' she explained, emphasising the sound of the letters. Intrigued by this little nugget of information, the little girls always remembered the sound made by the two alphabets — S and H.

To Conclude

You too can work out your own method of making the Flashcard Technique a breathlessly absorbing activity for your child. It will be a certain success due to the care you take to promote your child's curiosity and associations. And believe me, every minute will have been worth it. You will have sown the seeds of genius!

4

The Early Bird Catches the Worm

Education commences at the mother's knee, and every word spoken within the hearsay of the little children tend towards the formation of character.

Hosea Ballon

It has often been said that potential genius is closely connected to reading ability. To understand the significance of this sweeping statement, observe your own child carefully. From the time the child is born, he begins to live in a world of the five senses: sight, sound, touch, taste, smell. He may not do much beyond wailing or yawning, but he is already surrounded by conversation (mostly cooings and exclamations) and other sounds.

The Pictorial Visualiser

As the child begins to focus, he sees faces bending over him and disappearing, only to return again. His visual sense begins to develop. In this context, there is an interesting observation made by Owen Webster, a veteran reading instructor who, after fifty years of research, compiled his own rich experiences in an excellent book entitled *Read Well and Remember*. Webster states: 'Most people are predominantly visualisers, but the images they visualise most easily, are more likely to be pictorial than verbal.'

Initially, your child is a pictorial visualiser. Soon, in his infancy itself, he is ready for conversation, but all he can produce are baby sounds in answer to adult talk. The fact is that all his senses are ready and raring to go. But Mother Nature, in collusion with Father Time, prefers to proceed at her own steady pace. Wily as she is, she leaves it to you, the parent, to do your bit. You sing to the child and talk to him. The infant in turn, tries to mimic you by struggling to utter syllables and words.

Meanwhile, by your singing and talking, you are unwittingly, laying a solid foundation for the first phase of your child's life. He listens to you, hears the music and rhythm of language in your voice, and responds to it. Do you realise the import of that response? He responds because he is thinking. Soon, he tries to talk back to you, which means that he is learning to use his own voice. The more interaction there is between your child and you at this stage, the more talking and singing — the sooner will he develop his senses.

Linking Sight and Sound

From being purely a pictorial visualiser, your child is now developing his auditory senses. That means, he can now link sight and sound. It also means that the sooner he makes this link, the sooner he will develop his thinking prowess and speaking ability, and the sooner will he then be ready for reading. The essence of reading lies in the close interlink between the visual sense, the auditory sense and the ability to think.

How Does the Flashcard Technique Work?

The child's eye focuses on a word, for example — CAT. Instantly, a signal of recognition is sent via his brain like an efficient feedback circuit. It is processed, and the child utters the word — CAT. It may sound like a long, complicated process, but it happens in a flash of a few seconds.

What is the difference between a child pointing to a cat and uttering the word CAT and a child reading the word and saying CAT? The first example involves only a visual relationship — using a natural process to make the connection. The second example is a progression — development of an ability to make the connection. I have used the word 'progression' deliberately. It implies, 'a step forward'. At this stage, your child is still a pictorial visualiser, but he is also developing an important ability early on in life.

Imagine the plight of a person who cannot read. He knows a cat when he sees one. But when he sees the alphabets representing the same cat, to him, that is gibberish, or just some foreign-looking curves and lines that he just cannot connect with the flesh-and-blood animal that is licking its fur in front of him.

'That's a CAT?' he scoffs, pointing to what appear to be nonsensical scribbles to him. 'Now, that's a CAT!' he says, proudly pointing to the animal. He is unable to make the connection between the visual and the written word.

Let us take another example. A man named Raj knows that his name is Raj, but he cannot make sense out of the strange alphabets that make up his name. Raj, therefore, remains illiterate, and has to resort to a thumb print instead of a signature to identify himself. (He probably won't even recognise his own thumb impression if he sees it again!) His brain has remained undeveloped in this aspect. He can point his thumb at himself and say, 'I'm Raj, that isn't!', looking at the three alphabets in disgust. His mind is closed to learning!

Now, let us return to the child. At an early age, he is developing his natural ability. He can see the cat, and he can make sense out of those curves and lines that constitute the alphabets and word, and connect the two. It is a glorious achievement, a development that can never be underestimated. It is this extraordinary development that releases and feeds the genius that is inherent within him. It is already activating a powerful force within the child at an early age. He develops and makes connections. That in itself is an adventure — an extraordinary triumph over the ordinary. This ability also stimulates the child's interest in the world around him; it makes him develop a thirst for knowledge; it opens doors for the brain to develop, make connections, assimilate, and later, to analyse. It gives meaning to objects and words, and defines the link between them. It develops his superthinking powers early.

The Verbal Visualiser

Listening to your voice talking or singing has a deep impact on the child. He is eager to respond, to participate, and talk back to you. The responsive chord in him, the participator within, motivates him to communicate with you through the means you have already proved are available to him, that is — talking.

Articulating His Thoughts

It is important to develop his talking ability early because it is going to have a positive influence on his reading. Listening to his own voice acts as a powerful stimulator for the child. For example, as the word CAT escapes his lips, there is a delight within the child. He will, probably, not understand why. In actual fact, he is exploring his own potential. But, you, as an adult, have understood it. Also, it is a pleasure for you to hear your child talking. You may clap your hands spontaneously or communicate your delight to the child in some way. In turn he is delighted, and wants to repeat the action of talking over and over again. In effect, he is articulating or giving voice to his auditory senses.

The Appeal of Nursery Rhymes

Nursery rhymes play an extremely important role. They are irresistible and contain seeds of education that are invaluable. Their strong appeal lies in their catchy rhythm. Rhyming words stimulate the child's hearing and impart a great lesson: the ability to distinguish between two words. Consider the simple nursery rhyme:

> To market, to market, to buy a fat pig,
> Home again, home again, jiggety-jig!

Observe how the magic of this rhyme works on the child and develops his brain. Initially, he will enjoy the catchy, lively rhythm. He will begin to beat time to it. It will make him want to sing along with you. He may start singing falteringly at first, stumbling over words, and then find his confidence increasing. And as he does, he will develop his ability to make that fine distinction between the rhyming words — *pig* and *jig*. Isn't that marvellous?

Also, the constant repetitive quality inherent in nursery rhymes has the effect of embedding in him, simple words and meanings in an extremely enjoyable way. Simultaneously, repetition gives him constant practice of saying out words aloud. And as the old saying goes: Practice makes perfect.

Brain-Building at Home

The earlier a child talks, the earlier will the foundation be laid for development of his reading skills. After all, what is reading? I have already discussed how reading develops the ability to make connections. Now, let us analyse the basic meaning of reading.

Reading is *speech written down* or, more simply, it is talk in print. So when you encourage your child to talk, think of the tremendous potential you are releasing within him. You are, once again, making him use his natural ability of hearing. In turn, he articulates what he hears. This sets the wheels of stimulation whirring. He experiences a sense of achievement and wants to learn more and more to explore farther, the new phenomenon he has discovered! In short, by stimulating him early on in life, you are providing an impetus to his learning skills — you are awakening the genius in him. Once the wheels of genius have swung into motion, you must lubricate them with more and more knowledge.

When Anuradha Pandya was one year old, she sat at a table with her family. Her mother asked her to name everybody sitting at the dining table.

'Who's this?' her mother asked, pointing to the little girl herself.

'Anu,' said Anuradha.

'And this?' her mother asked, pointing to herself.

'Deepika,' the child replied, unhesitatingly.

'And this?' asked the mother, pointing to her grandmother.

The little girl hesitated, for the name was a bit of a tongue-twister by one-year-old standards.

'Ahilya,' prompted the mother. The child hesitated once more, but driven by her urge to communicate, said, 'Difficult.' A tongue-twister of a word in itself — *difficult!* It drew an appreciative laugh.

During the course of the meal, syllables of the word *Ahilya* were broken down and fed with every morsel she put into her mouth. By the end of the meal, little Anuradha was saying *Ahilya* quite easily! It was an achievement the little girl was proud of. And she wanted her mother to teach her some more tongue-twisters!

At the beginning of this chapter, I have mentioned the five senses. By now, you must have understood how they are inter-related. In a nutshell, you hold the key to developing your child's senses. Even though your child is not yet in kindergarten, you are already tapping his genius-ability by making an excellent start at home; by encouraging him to talk, to recognise words, to make connections. You are inculcating in him the interest to learn. And you are doing all these great and lasting things by stimulating his natural abilities and shaping them into the extraordinary abilities of a genius at an early age.

By your exemplary efforts, you are also extending your child's intellectual life. We have often heard the comforting homily: 'You have got your whole life ahead of you,' or 'You've got a lifetime to do this or that!' It's the greatest facility given to Mankind — a lifetime. If you begin your child's intellectual development early, you will extend his intellectual life and will be doing the greatest service to the child.

Recently, I read an article on fitness. The subject being interviewed was a senior advertising executive who is also a body-builder. To him, exercising every day is a must. Where most people eschew exercising due to lack of time, he says, 'If I feel I don't have the time, I just extend my day by rising one hour earlier.'

These seemingly casual words teach an invaluable lesson. The body-builder extends his day by waking up one hour earlier. This adds an extra hour to his day for body-building. Similarly, by starting your child early, you are adding extra hours to his brain-building life.

Extend Your Brain-Building Life

I am also reminded of some poignant words uttered by a 40-year-old fashion-designer. 'I wish I had been born 40 years old!' she said to me. She is a talented, hard-working bright young woman who was formerly working with Lufthansa Airlines. A change in her life made her switch careers. I will not dwell on that change as it is not relevant to this subject. But her new career opened up a new world. She was enthusiastic, interested, enthralled. She felt she was growing and developing. Her horizons were broadening. And her own satisfaction was making her a more secure person. She was also discovering new creative powers within herself. All these breathtaking discoveries made her say wistfully, 'I wish I was born 40 years old!' She was like a child who was watching and participating as her new career involved her in a continuously unfolding process.

Life indeed is just that — a never-ending, unfolding process. Obviously, the air hostess-turned-designer could not have been born 40 years old. But those wistful words revealed the regret of lost years and lost opportunities. The ifs of life ... if I had done this earlier.... The key word is *earlier*. By starting your child early, you are preventing him from falling prey to the *ifs* of life.

To Conclude

If you unfold and open out the exciting pages of your child's intellect early, you are extending his brain-building life. By making his senses work early, you are handing over to him, those extra, precious years that will make him, not just a genius, but a successful genius.

5

The ABC of Creative Inputs

*Of all the things that one may be blessed with, I can think of
nothing equal to the joy of having begot children who have grown
up to true enlightenment.*

Tiru-Kural

Making a genius is not just an art; it is a calling. Turning your
child into a genius requires you to always have a strong, positive
attitude towards intellectual pursuits. Since your child looks up to
you as the role model, you have to set his or her sights in the right
direction. You have to inculcate within the child, a deep, abiding,
healthy respect for knowledge. How much your child enjoys
reading is, to a very large extent, determined by your attitude
towards reading. For example, in his presence if you tell your
friend laughingly, 'As a child, I remember how I hated reading,'
this will have an adverse effect on him. I do not mean that you
should be walking on egg-shells all the time, but a little thought
before you utter such confidences, could show you where you are
going wrong.

On the other hand, if your child sees you absorbed in reading
the daily newspaper, or accompanies you when you visit the library
to select a book, he will realise that you like to read. He will then
want to follow suit. Since a child is naturally an artless and happy
little person, he will be very responsive to the idea of reading.

Also, his naturally insatiable curiosity, his sense of wonder and his perceptiveness will add to his enjoyment.

Your child is not yet of school-going age. However, you can help him develop his language and thinking skills at home. For that, you will have to follow some basic steps towards making a genius.

Books, Books and More Books!

Buy colourful, visually rich books for children. There is no dearth of such books in the market. To the child, they will be glittering goodies and he won't be able to wait to get his hands on them!

Read Aloud

Keep aside at least 15 minutes every day to read out aloud stories or nursery rhymes from these books. Apart from the intellectual value that this practice encourages (see Chapter 4), there is a great advantage derived from these cosy reading sessions. You build a warm, close relationship with your child.

Reading aloud works at more than one level. On the one hand, your child is deeply involved and contented at receiving your full and complete attention. Being close to you gives him a sense of your sharing and caring for him, making him secure. On the other hand, he is rivetted by the story and is completely absorbed in it, wanting to know what happens next.

The best reading plan is the bedtime story one. Your child has had his evening meal, taken his bath, and changed into his comfortable night clothes. He is ready, responsive and all set to drink in the words you are about to read out to him. He may even wish to choose the story he wants you to read to him. Let him. He may choose the same one you read out aloud the previous night and the night before that. It does not matter. Repetition has its own value. The next evening, try reading out a new story.

At times, you may find the child getting restless. He may want you to skip the next few pages and end the story as soon as possible. Do not be discouraged. He is going through, what I call, a discontented, creative phase. He may want a new story. Or he may want you to switch to a nursery rhyme. Do it. Nothing is a waste. The main factor here is that your child should feel free to enjoy himself. For, with this enjoyment, will also come the joy of learning.

To make him feel that it is fun and games, you will, I'm afraid, have to call upon your acting prowess! The narration can be read in your own natural voice. But when it comes to the various characters, a deliberate change in pitch, tone and voice will not only help him get the feel of different characters, but also increase his sense of enjoyment.

Postponing is Bad

Never postpone the bedtime reading session. It undermines, both, the value of the child and the effect of the exercise if you postpone it because of a telephone call or visitors. I know of one parent who did not allow even an electricity failure to interfere with the reading session. He lit a dozen candles, and chose a book which had larger pictures and fewer words. I would not recommend such extreme measures though!

Why do I say that the read-aloud time should never be put off. It is because the child is an active participant from the beginning to the end in it. He holds the book with you, turns the pages.... Sometimes, he may turn back to verify a certain picture. Sometimes, he may recite a familiar line from an old favourite because there's a similarity with what you are reading to him currently. Or, he may point at a picture he has seen several times earlier, but find a new word to describe it. The read-aloud session is an activity that the child participates in fully. It is very important to him. By giving it its due importance, you are allowing your little genius to grow up with the feeling that reading books is vital; it is an enjoyable activity and one, which he would like to make an intrinsic part of his life.

Pictures, Words and Word-Combinations

Imagine that your child is in a mysterious land of shapes and sounds (which he is until he begins to read himself). He has to make sense of what he sees and hears. Like a detective on the trail of hidden jewels, he has to track down the clues strewn in his path. The clues, in this case, are pictures, words and word-combinations.

Pictures help him to recognise or identify the characters in the story. For example, a family of monkeys enjoying a holiday on the beach may have been named 'The Funny Family' by the author. Without pictures to guide him, the child may assume that Mr and Mrs Funny are people. Later, he will learn to pick up the finer nuances and characteristics of the monkey family.

Words give clues too. For example, if the story is set in the Antarctic, the child could assume it is a place like any other. But after you have explained about the harsh, cold terrain to him, the story will acquire an entirely new complexion.

Word-combinations are normally artistic expressions of the author to give a poetic touch to language. They provide an evocative description that has a strong appeal. For example, when George Elliot writes about *dew-beads,* the visual image created in the child's mind makes the picture more vivid and meaningful.

Experience Adds Meaning

Teaching your child to read does not mean that you turn him into a stay-at-home bookworm. Far from it! Reading is like a two-way street with traffic coming in from both sides. The author and artist, together, fill the pages with exciting, creative ideas and stories through words and pictures. The little reader is not a passive passenger. He relates to these words and pictures with his own ideas and experiences. What he imbibes from the printed, illustrated page, will also depend on what he brings to it.

You may observe this yourself in your child. For example, your baby may have played with your neighbour's cat one evening. When he sees the picture of a cat, he will instantly squeal or coo with delight. His personal experience with your neighbour's cat will add more meaning to the picture than if you had shown him a picture of a kiwi, for example, which he may never have seen.

It is vital to understand that for the child-genius, experience adds meaning. Which is why, you should take the child out from a very young age. Take the child to the park, the zoo, the aquarium. Do not stop at that. Let the child accompany you to the bank, the post-office, the shopping centre, the supermarket or any other place you may visit.

Some privileged parents can take their children out of town. Sight-seeing trips are a treasure of information, whether it is seeing the Gateway of India in Mumbai, the Eiffel Tower in Paris or any other outstanding architectural feature in different places. Always remember to pick up brochures, postcards and books on these places.

When you reach home, have an animated discussion with your child. Encourage him to discuss his experiences and his ideas relating to these places. Ask him what he liked, what he disliked. You can make him refer to the literature you've picked up or the photographs you have clicked to give an added dimension to what he has to say. Make sure the discussion remains at an easy-going, informal, friendly level. If you sound like a cross-examiner in court, the child is sure to clam up! The tight tone, the right pitch, the right degree of interest will encourage the child and help him or her to articulate his thoughts clearly. Articulating clearly is the hallmark of the budding genius.

Foster a Sense of Curiosity

Every morning, your child wakes up to a fresh day. To a child, yesterday and tomorrow are almost irrelevant. It is today that is important and to which he devotes his full attention. To him everything has a fresh appeal — a bee buzzing around a flower; the sun's rays peeping through a chink in the curtain; a stray pebble on the pavement.... He is fascinated by people, their expressions, their way of talking and laughing. On the whole, life is one big, magical, exciting adventure in which he is an eager observer and participant.

With his little brain so full of ever-new discoveries, the child is prone to voicing aloud his thoughts, and wondering about things, places, animals and plants. Encourage him when he does. It is part of the growth of the genius-brain. For example, three-year-old

Anu surprised her mother one day with a statement that showed her acute observation and analytical powers.

'Mummy,' she said, 'do you know why windows are called windows?'

'Why?' asked her mother.

'Because the wind blows through them,' replied the little girl!

Play Word-Games

To a child, words are fascinating because of their mystery and sound. Learning a new word is an exciting adventure for the child. Subsequently, he or she will keep on using the new word all day, in every sentence, just for the pleasure of feeling it roll off the tongue!

You can increase the child's pleasure by playing rhyming, alliterative and guessing games with words. Nursery rhymes serve

a useful purpose when it comes to words that rhyme: Little Jack Horner sat in a corner; Little Miss Muffet sat on a tuffet; or words that begin with the same letters — Baa-Baa Black sheep or Jack and Jill.

Farozan Warsi devised her own word-games for her two daughters. For example, she taught them the *punished alphabets* in words. T is silent in Mother because the day that word was made, T was naughty and was punished. The two little girls were enthralled, and wanted to find out all the words in which a particular alphabet had been naughty and had been punished!

Sounds fascinate the child. I know of one parent whose many word-games included asking his children to name words that imitate sounds. The ensuing sounds must have sounded like a Diwali get-together or a Christmas party! — Bang! Pop! Whir! Splash! Tinkle! Ting-a-ling! Crash!

'We had a great time!' the father remembers.

Such imaginative games add a certain flavour of fun to the whole educational process. Consequently, the child is always interested and enthusiastic about learning more, and these are the signs of a genius.

Songs as You Go Along!

Research is still being carried out on the positive effects of music. Music can inject adrenaline or soothe. A case in point of its soporific quality is the lullaby that you croon to your child to put him to sleep. On the other hand, a catchy tune has him swaying, and later, dancing to its lively beat.

Music has a very important place in the world of the child-genius, not only because it is rhythmic and enjoyable, but also because, to a large extent, it is oral literature set to tune. Old folk songs have certain historical and cultural connotations in them.

The child also develops his musical sense by listening to good music. Initially, he begins by imitation. Soon, however, he is able to identify the source of familiar sounds and predict what sound to expect next. With its evocative power, music seems to link happenings. For example, on hearing the signature tune of a sound track, the child is able to identify the television programme that is about to be aired.

The era of therapeutic music is still in its infancy. In India, a university has been set up in Madras to conduct extensive research on the curative effects of music. Who knows! If your child-genius becomes a doctor, he may, one day, be using *musical remedies* as one of his prescriptions!

Why, What, When, Where, How?

The earlier the child learns to talk, the earlier he is bound to ask questions. He will bombard you with queries which are certainly going to make you feel like a war victim. Do not, however, discourage him, for this is an integral part of his growth and an indication of his eternal search for knowledge. Answer his questions as simply and completely as possible. If you don't know the answer, tell your child honestly, 'I don't know, but I will look it up and tell you.' Ensure that you follow up with action. Encourage the child to look up the answer with you and then, read it to him.

In fact, encourage the child to ask questions by always giving him or her your full attention. Your interest will generate his interest. A priest once asked me, 'What is the most important thing in this world for all of us?'

'Prayer,' I guessed, eyeing his robes.

'No,' he said, smiling gently. 'It is learning how to live.'

That is exactly what your child is doing — learning how to live. From a young age, you must fill him with the shining pearls of knowledge. They will glisten within him all the time and he will keep on asking with persistent curiosity: 'Why? How? What? When? Where?'

Vocabulary-Building from Everyday Life

Vocabulary-building from a young age is very important because it tickles the learning appetite of the child. It also gives him extra words to be able to articulate better. It adds to his reading pleasure. There are several interesting and exciting ways of building up the child's vocabulary. In fact, the means are all around us in our everyday life.

Encourage your child to talk about the things he has seen. For example, talk about that cat next door and ask him what colour he is. Is he white? Grey? Black? Is the colour of his eyes green? Is his fur soft?....

On your many outings, you can make him pick rocks or shells on the beach. Discuss the shape, size and colour. On the way to the market, he may spot a bird or a squirrel. Window displays are also good sources. Your child can be a window-word shopper! He or she will love this game. For example, when you reach home, you ask, 'What does the window-word shopper have in his word-shopping basket today?' Tea boxes, billboards, hoardings, newspaper headlines, the television screen — they are all good sources by which your little word shopper can increase his vocabulary. For example, the news on television makes repetitive use of words related to politics such as prime minister, president, nation; on the weather report — conditions, humidity, rainfall, sunny, cloudy, and so on.

Exposure to words builds up superthinking. The child will soon be able to graduate from *bow-bow* to dog, to *poodle* or *boxer*, from *flower* to *rose, sunflower*.... Each new word will help the word-specialist to express himself more lucidly. Each new word will make him want to learn one more new word. It's a snowballing effect in the best sense.

46

For example, a child was trapped in an automatic elevator during an electricity failure in Mumbai. She came running up to me later and said proudly, 'I was *rescued* by the liftman!' Not saved, not helped — but *rescued!*

One parent used an innovative idea for her little daughter. Since every doll or toy had a name, she made flashcards with the name of the doll written boldly on each: Meera, Barbie, Marie, Teddy, Choo-Choo, and so on. Also, the little girl's room had several cards all around depicting what each item was: My books, my bed, my window....

Our everyday life is full of colourful, vibrant, educative possibilities — use them for the little genius!

One Word, Many Meanings

As your child grasps words, encourage him to seek different meanings of the same word.

On one of those rare occasions that I found time to relax, I was enjoying a quiet Saturday evening at the beach. Not far from me was a family. The children were building a palace-hotel, as I gathered from their chatter. At the end of their efforts and the final patting-down, they gazed at it proudly. They had gone into great detail over it. The hotel, apparently, had air-conditioned rooms, gardens, water-tanks....

Then the naughtiest one of them, a boy of about four, ran his finger through it, ruining it. He announced, 'The garden is gone. There's no water. It's finished because the workers are on strike!' The loud protests would have probably ended in fist fights. But the mother, obviously, a wise young woman, quelled the protests by engaging them in a new game.

'Ajit,' she announced, referring to the little destroyer, 'has used a word — *strike*. Now, which of you can tell me, in how many ways can the word *strike* be used?'

The game proved to be absorbing as each child came out with his or her contribution.

'*Strike* a match!'

'*Strike* ten!'

'*Strike up* the band!'

'*Strike* Ajit with the ruler!'

To this, the mother added her own: '*Strike* a balance. Does it *strike you?*'

Such games enrichen the child's understanding of his vocabulary. Vocabulary-building is an excellent exercise for the budding genius.

To Conclude

Some parents are worried about *over-learning*. But remember, over-learning is a state of mind. If one parent stokes gently at the fire in the young genius-brain, the other should not prod at it vociferously and vehemently. This confuses the child and makes him or her feel that something is wrong. Like a good gardener, you have to tend lovingly to the budding brain. And if the child feels it's all one big game, he will flower out naturally into a genius.

6

The Magic of Storytelling

What was wonderful about childhood is that anything in it was a wonder.

G.K. Chesterton

Storytelling is a superimportant stepping-stone in genius-making. It brings alive the superthinking powers of a genius and releases the springs of his imagination. According to child psychologists, a child's mental growth proceeds at a rapid, breathtaking pace upto the age of six. Till the child is six years old, his learning power gallops like a horse on the race course. After that, it settles down to a steady, sustained ascent.

Before education was packaged into an institutional formula, it was the parent or the grandparent who was the teacher. Education was indirectly, but meaningfully, imparted in bygone eras through storytelling. Groups of children sat around fires and under trees, as the adult wove tales that gripped and absorbed them. Later on, as the printed word impressed itself on this traditional oral literature, it spawned the genre of fireside tales in the west or Grandma's *Gupshup* in India.

Storytelling has important ingredients in it which are extremely vital for the budding genius. Until the age of six, the very pattern of the brain, as designed by Nature, causes the child to have an insatiable curiosity to explore his surroundings physically. The child explores your face, runs his little hands over your cheeks, eyes, nose and mouth. A little later, he does it to himself. Every object, whether it is a toy or a speck of dirt, attracts his attention. He or she also experiments with cosmetics carelessly strewn on dressing tables. He pushes his little feet into your 'giant' footwear! It is all part of the 'great discovery'! This is the age when he is a traveller, rambler, trekker, sight-seer, voyager, adventurer ... everything rolled into one. Nothing is too lowly for him. Everything is meant to be picked up, examined, shaken, turned upside down.... If there ever was a live synonym for the word *explorer,* your child is a living example of one — a toddling, walking, talking explorer!

The little explorer is equally fascinated and mesmerised by a blade of grass as he is by a rusty nail, a stack of bright red apples or a heap of garbage. Everything is new in his world — the twittering of sparrows, the purr of a car engine, the pitter-patter of rain, the thundering of a train on tracks....

Enid Blyton, one of the most widely-read authors of children's books, was blessed with a rare talent to bring alive this world — which is why, generations have been fascinated by her stories. She captivated the essence of a child's world when she entitled one of her books *The Enchanted Wood.* Or take Lewis Carrol's *Alice in Wonderland.* These titles spell out the magic of a child's world. Most story-books carry within them the recipe for an enchanted childhood.

Storytelling, therefore, is a must for genius-making. Its power can never be underestimated. Stories are written by adults who have understood the child's world. These stories contain a power that is intangible but absolutely real. They help the child by opening out a world that is chock-full of enthusiasm, exhilaration and joy. But let's look at the tremendous advantages of storytelling one by one.

Stimulates Thinking Power

All good stories have good plots. For young children, the storyline should be linear since too many sub-plots or characters can confuse him. Stories should convey messages of hope, love and achievement, but without sermonising. The first objective that good storytellers keep in mind is — to tell a good story. At the simplest but most effective level, it has the *And Then?* quality. *What happens next? Where does he go? What does he do?* As the plot unravels, the child is carried away by its pace, its robust excitement. When the climax is reached, the child is delighted. Most often, he wants you to read out that story again and again. He knows the ending, but that does not diminish his interest. Soon, he is able to catch you if you make a slip. He tells you what will happen next. He grows and develops with the stories. A story stimulates and stirs his thinking powers.

Creates Visual Awakening

What happens when you go to the movies? The screen is filled with colour and movement. The visual clarity, the almost real-life characters grip your total attention. Storytelling has the same effect with a big difference — a very important difference that is essential to the budding genius. The strong, evocative words, rich in description, open up an inner-movie in the child's brain. He sees vivid pictures flashing in his mind's eye. Rudyard Kipling has created this visual magic with his pen in his rich, evocative prose with phrases such as: 'Beating of bullocks and creaking of wheels, lighting of fires and cooking of food.' The child instantly conjures up the lively scene, full of bustling activity in a camp. Added to that, the child's creative senses are awakened to visual possibilities. His imagination can interpret 'lighting of fires' to mean that it is dark. Or, of course, it could be a midday meal with the sun blazing down. And with these vivid images — the inner movie-reel that he spins out for himself — the child is developing a powerful visual sense.

Relates Words to Pictorial Images

Here is where your vocal acrobatics come in handy! A quavering, soft voice for an older person, a deep growl for the lion, a high, nervous chatter for the monkey ... in effect, you actually bring alive the words so carefully selected by the author for their phonetic quality. Apart from the listening pleasure and delight of your child, you are also sharpening his hearing to the finer nuances of sounds. Words become fascinating when they are delivered with different intonations and expressions. You can even add gestures to your dialogues. They will captivate the child, and trigger off the fun element of this educational process. Sounds add depth to the visual senses, giving an extra dimension to the child's *inner movie*. Kipling has captured the sheer exhilaration of words rolling off a tongue in *How the Leopard Got His Spots*.

The leopard comes up to 'a great, high, tall forest full of tree-trunks all esclusively speckled and sprottled and spottled, dotted and splashed, and slashed and hatched, and cross-hatched with shadows.' The rhythm of his words is so compelling that you will find your voice ascending and descending with the momentum he has, so artistically, conceived. And believe me, your little genius is not going to be speechless with delight! He will want to catch the rhythm of those words, say them aloud, and make them his own! It is like riding on a roller-coaster of words as he plunges in and out of them, absorbing them into his eager-beaver brain!

Develops Visual Imagery

By telling your child stories, what are you doing? You are transporting him into a mystical, magical world — a world full of changing scenes and splashed with brilliant, exotic colours.

Everybody has heard of the famous peacock dance in India. When it rains, the peacock spreads out his feathers in one big, glorious, fan-like flourish, revealing a profusion of blazing colours; radiating its joy in a triumphant, purple panoply as he dances in the exhilarating shower of life.

That is what you are doing to your child. As you weave in and out of these stories, his visual imagery flowers and flourishes. Like a well-tuned instrument, the child's brain vibrates to every experience. Even though he cannot personally experience each story or be each character, through stories — he sees lambs cavorting, gazelles prancing, doves swooping....

And when the little genius starts to read on his own, he colours the written word with all the images, sounds, gestures and experiences that he has imbibed. Experiences add the third dimension which is so vital to the young genius.

At an early age itself, the child may indicate his interest in specific topics — something that holds his interest; something that beckons him and makes him leave his favourite toy in its pursuit. It could be that he is fascinated by cars and peeps through the window at an endless procession of them. It could be a wildlife serial on television. Whatever it is, keep your own antenna alive and alert for these interests. Buy books on these subjects to show and read to him. You will be targetting two goals with one arrow: cultivating his interest in the subject, as well as channelising his enthusiasm into reading. It is an approach that will pay great dividends for the genius.

Nurtures an Understanding of Others

You want your genius to be full of useful knowledge that he can apply to his understanding of others. Storytelling provides just that. The characters come alive from the pages of a book, and through your excellent reading ability, the child distinguishes different characters, and even identifies with them. Each character becomes his friend. He may prefer one over the other. That doesn't matter. But from a very young age, he understands different characters. They are as alive, as real to him as you, his parents, are. And in understanding them, he begins to understand himself. This is a gradual process of growing up. With his discerning little mind, he will accept the fact that the naughty monkey is different from the fierce lion. Or that the peaceful dove is poles apart from the preying vulture. This will be an invaluable lesson for the genius as he grows up. He will learn to respect differences, and that will give him a broader horizon, as also, a perspective about himself.

Folk Tales Reveal Diverse Cultures

Folk tales are basically a portrayal of a culture through narration. They are an expression of the attitude and behaviour pattern of people from different parts of the world. By relating folk lore, you are adding to the genius' rich treasury of knowledge. Besides, folk tales are simple, with an inherent poetic quality. They tell of

people, who were closer to nature and their culture before urban living leavened us all into one faceless identity. The sheer diversity of cultures with their value system so intrinsically interwoven, all have an educational magic of their own. Here again, you can add to the child's enjoyment by adding slight regional flavours to your dialogues — the Chinese sing-song lilt, the Frenchman's soft t's, the American twang, the Britisher's clipped accent. They will provide a taste of international living for the young, budding genius!

Inspiration from Other Personalities

You want your child to be an all-round genius. You want him to do well in all subjects. You want him to score high marks. The best way to arouse his interest is to tell him colourful stories of great people who have played an important part in our world. You will find examples in every sphere: history, science, mathematics, music; even road-building, railways, and so on.

History, by its very nature, is full of heroes. But you also get children's books with short biographies of scientists, musicians and mathematicians. Geography can be enlivened by stories of great explorers such as Christopher Colombus.

This method is an excellent beginning for the genius, a launch-pad to actual studying. At a young age, the child will identify with people. By using this people-factor, every subject will become interesting. For example, what would a pre-school child understand about the laws of gravity? But try telling him that a great scientist called Newton was hit on the head by an apple and ... the entire scientific process will take on a different complexion — a human face!

The lives of great people also serve as a source of great inspiration to the child. By telling him their stories, you will put him in touch with the world of genius. It is a great start, an excellent take-off point for the genius to flap his wings in a rarefied atmosphere. It adds that *extra-ness* to the child — pointing him to the right direction; filling him with an enthusiasm and motivation that will give his genius that extra push.

Recapitulation Develops Analytical Skills

While stories in themselves are a great source of stimulation, a fun discussion at the end goes a long way in genius-making. Without sounding like a sergeant-major, you can gently draw out from your child all that he has imbibed. For example, you can ask him,

'What did you think of that baby elephant — what's his name?' The child is sure to supply the answer readily! It doesn't matter if you appear dumb. The child will delight in the role-reversal — where he is the teacher and you, the student. Educationists stress on the fact that the child should never be made to feel that he is slow or lacking in anything. A feeling that he is cleverer than you, on the other hand, will give him the impetus to go on. Of course, you will have to keep a fine balance, otherwise, the child may feel that he is too clever for you!

You can even use his favourite toy to draw him out. Tell him: 'Teddy says he doesn't understand why the baby elephant wanted to fly. Can you explain the reason to him?' In this way, you can elicit the entire story, the characters, the hows and whys from the child. This will develop the analytical part of his brain early on in life.

As he discusses the story with you and Teddy, he will also discipline his mind and, unwittingly, develop the logical process that is a must for a genius.

To Conclude

Storytelling unlocks those vast reservoirs of greater energies and creative ideas that are locked inside your child. It makes something flicker in the child. That tiny spark has the flame of genius in it. It glows in a world filled with great possibilities.

7

Creating a Superhome

What we learn through pleasure, we never forget.

A. Mercier

All of us are familiar with the old saying: *Home is where the heart is.* That is absolutely true. Home is where we find love, security and warmth. The home is the heartbeat of our life. It is where we grow and flourish. And never forget, that the genius home is where the heart of learning is. You may be wondering whether I am about to suggest turning your home into a university or a temple of knowledge. 'How grim and boring,' you would say. Far from it! I believe in fun. Not only because of its intrinsic quality, but also because I feel that fun is a positive element. It releases enthusiasm which, in turn, propels the need for knowledge and the will to seek it out, resulting in — you've guessed it! — a genius! Wasn't it the great German philosopher, Nietzsche, who said, 'Nothing ever succeeds which exuberant spirits have not helped to produce'?

However, home is not the only centre of learning. Equally important is the school, where the child learns to interact socially and imbibes knowledge.

Encourage Your Child to Go to School

Lekha Raman hated school. 'I had to be almost dragged to kindergarten every day,' she remembered. 'Once there, I'd refuse to go into my classroom. Stubbornly, I'd stand outside and cry.'

When Lekha became a mother, seeing the playful little bundle next to her, she made a vow: 'I'll never put my daughter through such torture.' She read every parent's guide she could lay her hands on. Somewhere along the line, she admitted, 'I realised that there had been nothing wrong with my school. It's just that the sudden change from the home environment to a strange new one was too drastic for me to take.'

Armed with her own insight, Lekha decided to ease her daughter's 'expected school blues' by creating an atmosphere at home that would make her look forward to attending school.

'Excellent idea!' I applauded. 'How did you do that?'

'To begin with, I always spoke about the school and the classroom as a happy place. I'd point to older school-going children and say, "Imagine, one day, when you are a big girl, you too will go to school! Won't that be fun?" Then, I converted one corner of her room into a kind of a study-place. I arranged all her dolls in a row and told her that they were her students. I bought a blackboard and chalk.

Then, one day, I read in a parents' guide about a teacher who writes on the blackboard:

> We will read stories
> We will play outside
> We will go to lunch
> We will sing.

Since my daughter was the principal of her school, I'd start her day by chanting these words to her. Then, I'd leave. And I'd hear her chanting these words to her dolls!

'And did she take to school?' I asked.

'Like a duck to water!' Lekha smiled.

Years later, Lekha's strategy and words have remained stuck in my mind. *Like a duck to water* — what an apt phrase! To turn your child into a genius, you have to make him take to school like a duck to water.

So far, we have concentrated on laying the foundation for a genius. But alongside, you have to set up the plinth. Many parents feel, that after an initial resistance, children take to school naturally. Yet I know of several adults who still abhor the idea of school and are happy that their school-going days are behind them.

If you want your child to be a genius, you cannot afford to let him think this way. If he hates school, that means his mind is full of negative learning.

I've actually seen this in practice in a joint family. (The names of the family members have been changed to protect their

identities.) Shikha has a daughter called Ambika, whom she dotes upon. Right from a young age, Shikha has fostered the idea in little Ambika's mind that school is a fun-place to go to.

Meghna has two sons — Ram and Shyam — whom she too loves and dotes upon. But Meghna hated the thought of her two little, 'vulnerable', fun-loving boys going off to school and being turned into 'serious students'. She felt she was curbing them. Since it was inevitable, however, she sent them off to school reluctantly, with tears in her eyes.

Shikha's and Meghna's families live in the same house and share the same environment. Ambika loves school; is ever-eager to learn; gets an exemplary report card every year; and excels in everything she does including music, sports, elocution and other extracurricular activities.

On the other hand, Meghna's two sons have to be forced to do their homework. They go to school reluctantly; they hate exams; their report cards are average.

Unconsciously, Meghna has passed on her negative attitude and curbed her sons' learning powers. Ambika, on the other hand, is flowering into a genius, due to her mother's positive attitude.

You realise, therefore, how important your attitude is towards fostering a genius. It is your attitude that moulds the child; it is your outlook that permeates the atmosphere at home.

Begin with yourself — your way of thinking. Affirm to yourself that school is fun and essential for your child's growth. You may see him off every day, but he will return home, sparkling and bubbling, and wanting to tell you everything he has learned and experienced.

On the other hand, even if you don't have Meghna's over-protective attitude, don't be indifferent. Never take it for granted that habit will endear your child to school. It may or it may not.

If you want the best for your child, wouldn't you want to see him looking forward to school, going off happily with his little tuck box in his satchel? Follow Shikha's example and make your child feel that school will be fun. Tell him that he will have plenty of playmates. And as Lekha put it to her child: 'It will be a place where the teacher will read stories; where children will play and eat; where they will sing. Remember, for the child — life is one big, happy playground.

Meanwhile, the home can be turned into a fun-filled environment, where learning together can be informal but stimulating. The atmosphere and activities provided can tune your child towards superlearning. What could be more fulfilling, more fun than that! All you need, with the suggestions given below, is a dash of initiative and loads of interest.

Fill the Hours with Fun-Facilities

Stock up on colourful books, toys, games, pencils, paper, crayons, paint, clay, and audio and video cassettes. Such paraphernalia is vital for the budding genius. It will help him in his exploration. Like an adventurous mountaineer needs his pickaxe to hammer out toe-holds on steep, slippery slopes, and his rope to help him climb up, so does your child need his tools to help him in his ascent towards sharpening his mental abilities.

Beads and Blocks

The child has to learn by doing things for himself. For example, give him uncooked macaroni or beads or blocks with holes in them. (At first, you may have to spend time convincing him that they are not meant to be put in the mouth!) By stringing these items, he will develop his hand-eye coordination. Sit with him while he does it. Don't do it for him. As he strings the first one, express your approval. That will stimulate him to go on.

A biggish truck and square blocks of different sizes are instruments for muscular coordination. The child will attempt to load the truck with the blocks. By trying out various ways, he will discover that the bigger ones take more space than the smaller ones. He will also discover that if the bigger ones are placed below with the smaller ones above, they will balance better and not topple over at the first push. As he moves the truck and blocks around, he will improve his muscular coordination. All these absorbing activities will build up his concentration.

Finger-Painting

Finger-painting may be messy, but your child-genius will love it! Why? For one simple reason: it feels good! It will hold his interest and give him a sense of power. He will dip his fingers into the paint and slither them across on the white paper, hesitatingly, at first. But as he sees the bold colours streaking across the page, he will want to continue. Up, down, right, left, circle, up and down

... what a glorious, exhilarating, powerful feeling to see the lines, splotches and splashes that he makes! His new-found confidence will grow as he splashes around some more! You can follow up by allowing him to use brushes or crayons.

Clay and Plasticine

Pre-school is also a good time to introduce your child to clay or plasticine. By playing with it, the child will get a feel of the moist, malleable substance. He will find, to his eternal fascination, that he can mould it into any shape. Since many children are hyperactive, clay-play channels their excess energies, and — in some cases — a latent aggression towards creative pursuits. And who knows, your genius may, someday, create a new spaceship!

Reading and Writing

Encourage your child to read and write. Draw letters and numbers and ask your child to copy them down. A word of caution — here is where the activity can take on a dull hue. So remember, make it like a game. But make sure, he writes alphabets by making the strokes in the right direction.

Initially, the crayon or pencil may slip from his tiny fingers. At such a time, you can use magnetic boards to help him learn his alphabets and words. Gently place the crayon in his fingers; place your hand over his and guide him over the page. When he sees the alphabet or number appear on the sheet, he will want to do it on his own. Don't be surprised if he throws aside your hand impatiently!

Most parents encourage their child to trace alphabets or pictures. But I would discourage such a practice. It hampers the creativity of the child and curbs his confidence — two ingredients that are so vital in the making of a genius. For the same reason, I would discourage colouring books with their ready-made outlines.

Following restrictive outlines means that the child will press down hard on the page and feel frustrated if his crayon goes out of the pattern. The genius must create for himself.

Reading is, of course, a must. Buy as many books as you can. If you surround your child with books, he will have a vibrant, colourful, exciting world all around him. I won't dwell on this subject as I have already dealt with it at length in the previous chapters. But this is the right time to start building up the child's personal library. Encourage him to share his books with other children. In time to come, let him accompany you to your library and select his own book to read. Being allowed to select a book of his choice — a book that interests him, will give him both confidence and satisfaction.

Subscribe to a children's magazine. By having the postman deliver a large cover with the child's name printed on it, you are telling the child: 'You have your own identity, a right to your own magazine. Here it is.' Encourage him to write letters to the editor, participate in contests, and later — write articles, poems, and so on. A budding genius must get an all-round exposure.

Audio and Video Cassettes

Audio cassettes are a great help to the child. He gets to hear the appropriate diction, the way a sentence is to be delivered. The advantage here is that you can even put on the cassette when he is having a bath.

Video and television programmes are also a good source of information for the child. They provide education disguised in entertainment — an irresistible mix! Viewing the dramatisation or animation of a story may spur him on to reading it. However, do not allow his TV or video-viewing to exceed ten hours a week. Never replace books with a video cassette. A book, as I have said earlier, opens the doors to the child's mind — making him imagine beyond what he sees in the static picture. That does not happen with a video cassette which spoonfeeds his inner eye, not allowing his mental growth to proceed at the pace it should. Video cassettes should be treated as additional facilities and appendixes to learning, not as the sole source of information. Since video-viewing is addictive, be careful. It is the video age, the visual age. But the printed word is still king in the land of mental growth. The genius can have his video cassette; but he must have his books and read them too!

Shower his Efforts with Approval

A well-equipped home without an atmosphere is like coffee without coffee powder! You will have to create that much-needed ambience of happiness and enthusiasm through your fun-to-learn attitude. And to make it extra effective, you will have to show your approval in bucketfuls. Yes, indeed! Your little genius needs your approval constantly. It is a relatively inexpensive commodity and requires little effort on your part.

As an adult, with your own childhood far behind you, you have, probably, forgotten how cheated you felt if your parent barely glanced at something you had worked so hard on. Don't make that mistake with your child. A smile, a nod, a pat on the head, a few encouraging words — all require little effort on your part. But to the child, it will make a world of difference. *It will* mean that he is successful!

Never put off seeing what the child has done and presented for your approval. If you do, you will dampen his enthusiasm. As the minutes or hours tick by, he will be seized with uncertainty about being successful. His confidence will be undermined. The next time, he may shy away from doing something or drag his feet over it.

Praise encourages the child to strive harder. He basks in the glow of your approval. A word of praise from you will make him feel worthwhile, and from then on, he will want to learn more.

There's Fun in Sharing!

There's a deep fulfillment in sharing — sharing your time, sharing yourself. Nothing can replace it — not the best books, the best toys, the best TV programmes, the best music system, the best computer. They acquire value only when your child can share them with you. When you share yourself with your child, you are participating in his activities. You are telling him that he is important, that everything he does is important. With that rock to stand upon, your child will develop a firm belief in himself and in his abilities, and he will respect himself. That will be the cornerstone from which his genius will blossom.

To Conclude

Your home is the place where you can condition your pre-schooler to look forward to school. Introducing him to the facilities he will encounter in school, will instil in him, a sense of confidence and familiarity with toys and games. He will await his entry into the next 12-year phase of his life with eagerness and excitement!

8

Like the Potter With the Clay...

Little strokes fell great oaks.

Proverb

In a drought-stricken area, a farmer turned his sunburnt face upwards. He watched unbelievingly as the clouds gathered. 'It must be a passing shower,' he murmured to himself, trying to stem the wild hope that was leaping within him. If the rain turned out to be a mere drizzle, he did not want to be disappointed.

In the same area, another farmer watched the clouds with satisfaction. He had been in touch with the laboratories and requested them to seed the clouds. His efforts were bearing fruit. He knew that the downpour would be heavy. He knew that it would not be just a passing shower.

If you were to choose between the two farmers, whom would you prefer? You'd prefer the second one, of course. His positive approach and educated efforts were about to fetch the best results — a heavy rainfall. He knew he would have a good crop that season. He also knew that in the seasons to come, he could try out more advanced methods to get better results. He was never going to put himself in a position where he would be murmuring, 'it must be a passing shower.'

In the same way, I am sure you do not want your child's genius *to be a passing shower*. You do not want the early promise to be reduced to the realms of the average. You want a sustained growth, not a one-season wonder. You want that early flowering to grow into a deep-rooted tree. You want the branches of the tree to be always overhanging with lush greenery, and flowers and fruit.

To attain all that, you will have to be like the second farmer — not seeding the clouds only once, but thinking ahead about how you can always have a good season. We've all heard about the strength of the positive philosophy that can move mountains. It's been encapsulated in three simple words: *Mind Over Matter.* It can be interpreted in several ways. In the earlier days, when it was coined, it was a definition of faith and belief. But in our more complex times, I think we should view it from a new perspective. We should give it a more active connotation: *Putting Our Mind Over Matter.*

This is what you should do: superimpose your mind over that of your child like the potter moulds the clay. Guide and influence your child towards a more active role.

In the previous chapter, I've dealt with creating a superhome for the genius, laying the foundation, setting up the plinth. Now it is time to move on. Your pre-schooler is shooting up — storey by storey. He needs your mind to mould him into a tall, strong skyscraper. Within your home, circumstances will change. Soon, the little genius will be going to school. Your approach will now have to be a little more sophisticated, a little more advanced.

You've already opened the portals to superlearning and superthinking. Now, it is time to stride through those sunshine-filled corridors. It is time to move on!

Sharpen Your Child's Intellect

In the modern world, there is every likelihood that both parents could be working. Keeping this factor in mind, and after much careful thought, research and my own experiences, I have suggested several simple ways and means by which you can sharpen your child's intellectual power.

Early to Bed ...

It is imperative that the budding genius gets his eight hours of sleep, so that his mind is always fresh. I know of one couple who was fond of throwing parties. Their two young children attended them too. After every late night, they had to be coaxed into waking up the next morning and going to school. Breakfast was a hurried affair before they rushed off to catch their schoolbus. Often, the two children even missed going to school. You cannot afford to do this with your child. Clear thinking is extremely essential for the little genius.

And Early to Rise ...

Rising early is a natural corollary to going to bed early. There's something magical about these hours, a peaceful quietness that stimulates the mind. Many authors say that they have written their best works in the quiet hours of the dawn. It's a wonderful habit to cultivate in the budding genius.

Exchange News and Views at Breakfast

Breakfasting together is a beautiful tradition. Every member of the family is fresh and looking forward to the day. It is also the time when you scan the newspapers. As your child sinks his teeth into his slice of bread, let him also bite into a loaf of news. Read out interesting bits of news and discuss them with him. You will be surprised at his insight or his way of interpreting the news. It's an excellent grounding for the young citizen of the Information Age.

Playtime is Learning Time

All work and no play will make the genius a dull child. Let him play with the neighbourhood kids. The neighbourhood environment is a great playground for nurturing social skills: he will learn to give and take, to face rejection and ridicule, to stand up for himself. He will learn the meaning of sportsmanship by experiencing the thrill of victory and taking failure as a stepping-stone to success. This interaction is a must for his growth.

Homework is Your Child's Work

Though it is good to spend 15 to 30 minutes over your child's homework to know what he is doing, *don't ever make the mistake of doing it for him.* I remember a satirical television serial called *Wagle Ki Duniya* — a brainchild of one of India's greatest cartoonists, R.K. Laxman. One of the episodes portrayed the misguided Wagles sweating and swotting over their son's homework and

studies as he played with his friends. The end had a classic touch, so typical of Laxman's perspicacious wit. When the boy brought home his report card, he was indifferent and rushed off to play again. Meanwhile, the parents pored over the report card, and slowly, a smile spread over their faces. The camera froze on the parents shaking hands, with beams of self-congratulations! *They* had obtained a good result! Self-satisfaction at seeing that your child has done well due to your efforts, is harmful for the child. Always let him carve out his own path.

Include the Day's Experiences in the Dinner Menu

There's an old saying: *A family that eats together, stays together.* To that I'd make two more additions: *A family that eats together, learns and grows together.*

The dinner table is a splendid platform for discussions. It's a time when your child can regale you with his day's experiences and achievements, including his lessons, play and friends. Listen to him attentively. Applaud his accomplishments. If he confesses to having made a bloomer, gently show him that it is human to make mistakes. He should not have such high expectations of himself that every little molehill of a mistake is built up into a mountain of disappointment and frustration. You can give him examples of your own bloomers committed in your childhood and laugh at them. This way, he will learn to laugh at himself.

Learning from his mistakes and learning to laugh at himself are vital stepping-stones towards becoming a genius. If these qualities are not injected at an early stage, the child can become a poor loser, and even cheat to get the expected results. To give you an example: Little Sandra always came first in class. Her parents were extremely proud of her. When it came to sports, however, it was a different story. Sandra was to participate in a rope skip-and-run relay. Knowing that her parents expected her to be a winner, she swirled the rope up and down as she ran, but never really skipped like the rest. She was disqualified. This had a tremendously negative effect on her. She cried and sulked for days. It took all her parents' patience to make her understand that they still loved her. Sandra came out of it, subdued. It was a terrible experience for her and an awful lesson for the parents. They had failed in their duties. Don't let that happen to your child. Remember, even a genius makes mistakes.

Stimulate the Brain for Dessert

After the table has been cleared, you can play cards, word-games or any brain-stimulating activity. You can teach your child to play chess — a game that requires the player to plan, analyse, think several steps ahead, and improvise according to the situation.

You can watch the news aired on television with your child. This is the time when the world comes alive to him or her. Encourage him to discuss his viewpoints and ideas on what he has seen.

Bed for the Budding Genius

Bedtime should be more relaxed. Here, you can read aloud a story. If your child, by now, can read for himself, let him. But be very firm that he sleeps early. Sleep is the time the brain recharges its batteries. Your child may be a potential genius, but he is also a child of nature. In this respect, he is like any other child.

So far, I've touched on how you can blend your daily activities into the educational process for the genius. Now, I'd like to concentrate on other areas that will set those little wheels in the brain of the budding genius rolling even more.

Provide a Special Work-Area

When your child starts bringing work home, he will need a place where he can sit quietly, without any distractions. If you have a large house with several rooms, he can have a den for himself. On the other hand, if you stay in a small apartment, turn a corner into his own little wonderland.

If you can afford it, buy him one of those lovely, little antique-style desks that opens outwards, and whose inside houses those exciting little pigeonholes, and nooks and shelves. If it doesn't fit into your budget, get an ordinary desk and chair or even a table with drawers.

Make sure that his workplace is well lit. You can also add other imaginative touches. For example, put up a cork notice-board. He can pin up photographs, newspaper cuttings, phrases — anything. You can also encourage him to write and pin up 'A Thought for the Day.'

A word of caution: discourage him from studying in bed or in front of the TV. This way, he won't be able to concentrate fully on his work.

Stock Ready References

It is never too early to buy reference books. They are excellent sources of information. Kept handy, they encourage the child to read and investigate for himself. He will also be proud to have his own Reference Library.

There are several excellent, well-researched books available in the market. They are bibles of knowledge.

Dictionary — Every day, add to your child's vocabulary by giving him a word to look up and learn. If he misspells a word, don't correct it for him. Gently ask him to look it up in the dictionary. The same goes for mispronunciation.

Encyclopedia — If you have read in the newspaper or heard news about a country over the television, encourage him to locate the country and read about it in his encyclopedia. It adds a depth of understanding to what he has heard and also to what he will be hearing over the next few days.

Since geographical boundaries are being redrawn in today's fast-paced world, let him make his own encyclopedia by cutting out news items and sticking them neatly in a scrapbook. To make it exciting, you can name it *The New Encyclopedia*.

The encyclopedia is also useful for finding out scientific, geographical, historical, biographical and cultural facts.

Atlas — Maps can be used to immediately locate the country or state that is in the news. But they also have other uses. If you are planning a family vacation out of town, ask your child to chart out the shortest road-route to your destination. On your drive, let him navigate. Similar methods can be used if you are travelling by rail or air.

Almanac — This worthy book is a rich source of knowledge, packed as it is with sports records, celestial events, weights and measures, postal information, facts about history, national parks, rivers, dams, and so on. For example, if an athelete breaks a world record in sprinting, encourage your child to refer to the almanac to find out about past records and events. It will build up his store of knowledge. Or, in this new world of environmental hazards, he can look up information on dams or oil-slicks. This will furnish him with applied knowledge that will come in handy.

There are several other books that you can buy for him, but these are the basic reference books that are a must for the genius' library. Initially, teach him how to use them. But never spoonfeed him by looking up the information yourself.

Monitor Radio and TV Programmes

Radio and TV are good sources of information as they animate the world for the child. He can see and hear in flesh and blood, people he has only heard about earlier. Encourage him to watch

educational programmes like word-quizzes, number-games and interesting documentaries. But do not let this interfere with his studying or reading.

From programme guides, select the shows you want him to watch or listen to every week. Prepare him for them. For example, a special documentary on whales could be preceded by reading a book on mammals, a trip to the aquarium or sketching the mammal. Even after the programme, encourage him to do follow-up reading and hold open-ended discussions. Challenge your child to consider if there is a bias in programming or if news reports are accurate. At this stage, your child's superlearning and superthinking abilities should be working hand in hand.

Cultivate the Art of Writing

You have provided your child with writing material. Simultaneously, cultivate in him the art of writing and penmanship. Remember, good writers are clear thinkers. They know how to arrange their topics in a certain order. As they write, they express new ideas. Learning to write well is an art in itself. It also inculcates the art of practice and patience. By combining this art and the science of writing, you are setting the field for good communication skills in your child. Effective communication skills are a necessity in this Information Age.

To Conclude

Let me, once again, reinforce what I have already said. That is: *You must set a good example to your child.* Remember, the child's world is an imitative reflection of yours. Whether he or she plays House-house or some other game, he is basically reconstructing what he has seen and experienced. Always try to use correct English and grammar when speaking. Let the child see you reading and writing. Remember — you are the potter who is going to design and shape the clay the way you want!

9

The Genius in Toyland

It is only through curiosity that children learn to understand the world around them; it is only through curiosity that science has progressed.

R.K. Narayan

Her appearance bespoke of good breeding. She was elegantly dressed. Every hair was permed and patted into place. I was contemplating her immaculately pedicured, varnished toe-nails, when she said, 'Please do come over to my place for a cup of tea.'

After some polite conversation and a 'cuppa', she took me on a conducted tour of her house. It was squeaky clean with every artifact wiped and polished to perfection and stacked neatly in its place. Then we entered her son's room. I was taken aback to see another sparkingly neat room.

'His toys,' she said proudly. I peered at the rows of gleaming wonders. 'I've taught him to be very, very careful with them,' she added. Not a single toy was chipped or broken. They looked so new that I could almost imagine that their wrapping was still intact.

'Doesn't he play with them?' I asked feebly.

'Of course, he does,' she answered in a suitably shocked tone. 'But he is very careful. He knows I can't stand untidiness. In fact, I think he takes after me.'

I looked at the smug complacence on her face, and felt a great sense of sadness and loss for the absent child. What a waste! What a monumental waste! I could have cried at the thought of the little boy probably never touching them, with the 'dragon of cleanliness' breathing down his little neck. I made my excuses quickly and escaped from the cloying, claustrophobic atmosphere.

That entire evening, I was a little depressed at the thought of all the joys and pleasures that that little boy was missing out on. The visit made such an impact on me that when I thought of writing this book, I decided to devote an entire chapter to toys. After that incident, whenever I see a house with chipped, broken toys lying around, reflecting an on-going, untroubled happy childhood, I heave a sigh of relief.

You see, I've always believed strongly in the power of toys. Every parent buys these little colourful objects, but very few realize the potential they have. Very few are aware that toys enhance genius potential by developing basic skills that are absolutely necessary for the genius.

Developing Basic Skills

Physical — When your daughter pushes or pulls along a doll's pram, is she playing Mother? Or when she skips and jumps on a rope, rides on a horse, tricycle or bicycle, is she just having a good time? The answer is Yes to both. But, in addition, she is also learning to walk, run, climb, jump and reach. It is not only good exercise; there is also a very important factor attached to it. She is developing her physical skills. By moving her limbs, as she has seen adults do, she is getting ready for a great, active, happy life.

Motor — She bends over puzzles ... with her little tongue sticking out, she colours her book with crayons.... Delightedly, she separates the pieces of the take-apart toy and carefully assembles them together again.... She constructs a house, she moulds the clay into a required shape.... By doing all this, the child is enjoyably and usefully developing her special motor skills: namely, hand-eye coordination, and finger and hand dexterity.

Visual — He plays catch with his red rubber ball ... with his racquet, he hits the shuttlecock across the net ... he tosses a ring over the protruding ring-holder and scores ... he flies a kite ... he operates the electric train or the road-racing fleet of cars.... In effect, he is enhancing his eye-movement skills and visual judgement because these activities require him to follow a moving object visually and make contact with it.

Visualisation and memory — He plays a board game like drafts or chess.... He sketches ... then sorts out differently shaped blocks and fits them into their matching hollows.... He is developing his visualisation and memory skills that are needed for comprehension. He is using his imagination. All these skills are essential for a genius.

Specific concepts — He shakes the pouch, puts his hand inside and draws out the square plastic objects, each with an alphabet on it. Then he constructs a word and arranges it on the board. Next, he pushes that aside and moves on to Monopoly, a board game. He counts the money, buys a hotel or a house.... He is playing games that have been designed to help him learn specific concepts such as actual formation of words or handling money.

Tapping Creativity

So far, I've touched only on the toy-playing aspect. But a budding genius has an innate curiosity to explore and exploit his/her potential to the utmost. Encourage the child to be a toy-maker. For example, your little daughter can use old cartons, caps, cans, containers, reels, pegs, strings, glue, and so on to make a car, traffic lights, pedestrians.... That car can experience many adventures, including falling off a bridge (made with her ruler) into a deep ocean (improvised by putting water into an old basin)....

Now, you may ask: 'Why should my daughter labour at this sticky, messy stuff, when I can get her well-made toys with which she can have similar adventures?'

The difference here is that you are awakening her creative genius. She is not only a viewer, but a doer. She is creating the situation. She is experimenting and improvising with material. She is formulating the rules with each new situation.

Sharing with Others

If she taps her creativity with a playmate, there will be added benefits. She will learn to share responsibility. She will learn the valuable lesson of making a *joint decision*. At the same time, she will learn to pool her knowledge with her friends, and learn a few technical terms. She will also learn how to get along with another child and be more responsive to her friend's needs. She will develop what social scientists call *interpersonal relationships*. For the genius, this kind of a supercreative toy-making-and-playing activity is a must.

81

Electronic Games

I've heard many parents decry the new-fangled video games. 'We didn't grow up on them and we aren't the less for it,' they say. But I think they are forgetting one simple factor even though it is staring them in their faces. They were born years ago in a different time. Since then, the world has changed. And your child faces this changed world. He is right in the midst of the New Information Age.

Events have moved so rapidly that information is pouring in from every corner of the world. Due to the vast reach of places and people he is becoming an international armchair traveller.

To you, Prehistoric means the age of the dinosaurs. To him, it could well mean Pre-World War II or even, Pre-television! To you, space travel was a science fiction story. To your child, *it* is a reality. Your childhood ambitions may have included becoming a pilot. His would include becoming an astronaut. Even today, you may feel silly talking to an answering machine installed by your friend. To your child, it will soon be a necessity.

Electronic learning aids, video games and computers are very much a part of your child's world. You must introduce him to them. This way, he will be prepared for the high tech Information Age he has been born into and will be stepping into professionally when he is an adult. Can you deprive your budding genius of these benefits?

Also remember, there was perhaps no remote-controlled television in your childhood. Perhaps you were not even allowed to touch the TV set. But now your child can change channels and lower or raise the volume at the touch of a button. Without realising it consciously, he is already getting a taste of power because he can control a machine by just pressing a button! That's one of the reasons why we find today's children more confident, more poised, more self-assured than we were at their age. Your budding genius is part of this process. So, depriving him of electronic games is the biggest mistake you can make.

Decision-Making

Whether it is an electronic or non-electronic toy, there is a basic similarity in both kinds. Both give the child valuable practice in decision-making. Let me elaborate. When your child holds a toy in her hand, the first thing she wants to know is how it works. Once she masters this, the next thing she ponders over is what she can do with it. She then develops her own ideas on how to play with it. Even at the simplest level, her doll can be her daughter if she is playing House-house, or her nurse if she is playing Hospital. By improvising games with her toys, by delegating roles to her toys, she is already practising decision-making. This is a valuable experience for the genius.

Be Your Child's Guide and Playmate

To derive the maximum benefit out of toys for your child, to guide your genius into Toyland, you will have to be your child's guide and playmate.

Be a child yourself — The childlike (not childish) parent can communicate better with his child and by doing so, make a more significant contribution to developing the genius potential.

Be active — *You* can encourage creativity by getting new toys and participating actively by playing with your child. Initially, you can introduce new play-concepts as a mind-setter. Let the child take off from there. This will help him to become more comfortable with new things and changing situations.

Introduce various activities — *As* an adult you have the maturity to perceive your child's individual needs, interests and abilities. It will be up to you, therefore, to introduce a variety of suitable activities. This can include physical activities such as jogging or gymnastics; verbal activities such as telling stories or jokes; and game activities such as charges or hide-and-seek.

Set an example — The best, most sophisticated toys in the world will not achieve the effect of developing the genius potential if you, the parent, do not set an example in the way you play with your child. It is your approach, your behaviour that the child will emulate.

Surround your child with love — It is only when your child feels secure in your love, when she feels enfolded in your care, that she will become independent enough to enjoy her toys and develop her creativity through them.

Where to Draw the Line?

Research conducted on parent-child-toy relationships has thrown up interesting findings. Children who play often become more creative and imaginative than those who have had a limited exposure to toys. Children who play regularly with their parents and others are most likely to achieve the highest level of creativity as adults.

You may, however, often be in a quandry about whether you are motivating the child through your participation in her play or whether you are interfering in her natural growth. You may wonder where to draw the line. To overcome this difficulty, try this exercise:

Observe — Watch your child's skill levels and play interests closely. Ask yourself: 'Do I belong?'

Play along — Play at your child's level. If your approach is too complex or difficult for her, she will become frustrated.

Introduce more complex games — Gradually introduce her to a slightly newer, more complex play-level. For example, you can first let her master a board-game like drafts. After she has mastered it, introduce her to chess.

Back away and observe again — After demonstrating a new concept and arousing your child's interest, back away. Let your child practise and learn on her own.

Re-enter — After she has mastered this new concept, you can re-enter the play-picture once again!

The above five points have been given only to prepare you at a psychological level. But don't lose your sense of fun and spontaneity by adhering too rigidly to them. Have fun with your child and watch her genius develop under your loving guidance.

Selecting Toys

A final word on toys. Obviously, the majority of parents are on a limited budget. You cannot afford every toy in the store, however tempting. Therefore, while selecting a toy, you must ensure that your child derives maximum entertainment as well as education from it. Variety is important. To make sure that your child gets a positive and maximum exposure to toys, while also ensuring balanced play of different activities, you have to be very selective. Keep the following points in mind while choosing toys. The broad parameters given below will help you to keep the balance-play aspect in mind when you walk into a toyshop.

Active Physical Play (APP) — This ensures a well-coordinated child. Exercise develops his muscles and body. Moreover, the active physical aspect that involves coordinating his movements into purposeful actions, develops his brain as well. Balls, tricycles, bicycles; sports equipment such as racquets, shuttlecocks, and so on are good examples of APP toys.

Creative Constructive Play (CCP) — This awakens positive creativity in the child. Creative toys allow your child to figure out how they work. They stimulate his observation powers and help him to develop new concepts and self-expression. Good examples of CCP toys are construction blocks, painting material, musical and scientific toys.

Imitative Play (IP) — Toys which can be used for imitative play bring out the original thinker in the child. Here, the child *make-believes*, which, in itself, shows that she is stimulating her imagination. By creating new situations she is also developing her sense of original thinking.

Dolls, stuffed toys, vehicles, aeroplanes, costumes ... are all good for imitative play.

Social Play (SP) — This activates the socially-skilled child. By interacting with other children, he learns about competition, sportsmanship, the ability to stand on his feet. It also inculcates concentration. Board-games, card and word-games, puzzles, outdoor games that are played on a one-to-one basis or in teams, are excellent for developing social-play skills.

While selecting a toy, think. Sometimes one toy can cover all the four aspects I have enumerated. For example, the Frisbee disc[1] involves:

- active physical play since your child has to toss it and then run to catch it;
- creative constructive play because your child can experiment with the many ways it can be tossed;
- imitative play since the child can imagine that he is the Frisbee champion of the world and play with that extra flourish;
- social play because he is in competition with other children.

---

[1] A concave plastic disc for skimming through the air as an outdoor game.

To Conclude

Toys awaken the mighty creative power within your child. By developing his physical and mental skills, you are giving him a great gift — to live magnificently and creatively, to live the life of a genius!

10

Stepping-Stones for Success

Good, better, best;
Never rest
Till 'good' be 'better',
And 'better' 'best'.

Nursery Rhyme

When Lord Rama wanted to cross the sea to Lanka, a path was laid for him. Enthusiastic helpers picked up stones to enable him to reach his destination. Every stone dropped into the waters brought him a step closer to Lanka. There is a great lesson in this for us. It is a shining example of what can be achieved. As Confucius said, 'The longest journey begins with a single step.'

Like Lord Rama, every child is standing on the shores of life. At his feet the vast ocean of knowledge surges and roars its mighty message. The child can conquer it by crossing three stones — three stepping-stones that will bring him to the Promised Land — the energising land of the genius.

The three stepping-stones are *creative curiosity, inspired imagination* and *independence.*

First, however, I'd like you to study your behaviour pattern with the child. Ask yourselves these questions and answer them with a simple YES or NO.

1. Your two-year-old tries to open a box full of biscuits. Do you reprimand him and take the box away from him?

2. Your child plays with mud and water. Do you exclaim in horror, promptly wash his hands, and seat him on the bed surrounded by *clean* toys?

3. While you are busy cooking, your child has unearthed some empty cartons. Hearing the noise, you rush to the scene. He is trying to reach a higher shelf for one more carton. 'No!' you shout. Do you pick him up angrily, place him in front of the television set, and switch it on?

4. If he sits happily watching cartoons, commercials or soap operas, do you look at him occasionally to say, 'Good boy!'?

5. If he rebels by trying to get off the chair, changes channels, or wanders around trying to find some distraction, do you sigh impatiently and push him back on his seat with a warning?

6. His inquisitive little fingers have found your lipstick. Wondering why he is so quiet, you look inside your bedroom, and gasp with horror when you see the red slashes on his face, his hands, his clothes. Is it time for another rebuke?

7. Your ten-year-old child shows you his work of art. All you see is a hotchpotch of colours drawn in squiggly lines. Do you give it a brief glance, murmur 'Good,' and go back to reading your book?

8. Do you look at a painting made by him and question him closely about it? 'What is it?' you ask him. If he says, 'A dog,' do you laugh and reply, 'That's not a dog!'?

9. One day, your twelve-year-old boy confides in you that he wishes to become a dancer or an actor. Do you get into a state of panic and exclaim: 'That's sissy stuff!'?

10. You find your six-year-old daughter playing with her elder brother's toy rifle or construction set. Do you take it away from her, saying, 'That's not for girls. Play with your dolls!'?

Now look at your score. To how many questions have you answered YES and to how many, a NO? Now, assess yourself:

1. If you have answered No to all 10 questions — you are the perfect parent for a genius! Keep it up!

2. If you have answered No to 7-9 questions — there's still hope for your child. You should work on the weak areas in yourself.

3. If you have answered No to 6 questions and below — you had better take a good long look at yourself and your attitude. You could be suppressing your child's genius-ability.

As you may have noticed, I have taken simple examples from our day-to-day lives. There will, of course, be variations of your reactions to these situations. Let us examine each set of questions and get to the core of your reactions. If you have answered NO to all ten without hesitation or qualification, you can skip the next few paragraphs. However, if you are curious, read on. On the other hand, if you are a YES parent, it would be a good time to examine yourself and see and understand what lies behind your reactions.

YES to Questions 1-5: You are busy. You don't want to be disturbed. So you find easy ways out to keep your child busy and out of your hair. That's your main reason.

YES to Question 6: Your sense of neatness and cleanliness is outraged. You are also fed up at the extra work it entails, that is — scrubbing him clean once again. As though you didn't have enough to do already!

YES to Question 7: Here you are deep in the middle of an exciting mystery story. The detective is about to....

'Dad, see what I've done!' O God! you hate to be disturbed — a brief glance — a nod of approval — and back to the detective novel!

YES to Question 8: You wonder what your genius has created today. What's this? Looks like scrambled eggs thrown all around! You feel that you had better set him straight.

I can understand your reactions as stated to Questions 1-8. They are human. They can also be corrected quite easily, depending on the openness with which you've approached this self-assessment exercise. You will realise that the fault lies not so much with your child as with you. Your busy schedule, your preoccupation, your expectations...

But if you've answered YES to Questions 9 and 10, believe me, your attitude will have to undergo a radical change. Your sexist approach is unhealthy and wrong. There's no rule in the world that says that girls and boys, by their very gender, have to play a particular role in society. A genius plays all the roles. He or she may specialise in a particular subject some day. But knowledge and experience helps in all aspects of life. If a boy plays with a doll, he could grow up to be a better paediatrician, for example. Or a

girl playing with a construction set could be a top scientist at the Space Centre. Moulding a child into a set pattern is stultifying. It is like the age-old practice of traditional Chinese parents binding their daughter's feet to keep them small and feminine. Such wrong perceptions and prejudices will bind the child's mental growth.

If you persist with such attitudes, by the time your child is old enough to understand, he will be more concerned about what others say about his work. He will pause before he does anything because he does not know whether he is doing something right or wrong in the eyes of society. In short, he will be afraid to show his originality or that he is different from the mould cast by you.

However, if you are ready to throw aside outdated thinking and behaviour patterns, you can work towards a great shining future for your child. You can chart out methods that will draw out your child's inner powers, his originality, his individualism.

Curiosity, Imagination and Independence

A genius is creative. But also remember, a genius is not just a highly intelligent person with a lightning-quick grasp on matters; he is unique in himself. He will carve out a unique role for himself in society and the world. To awaken his great creative powers, let him set out on the three stepping-stones mentioned above.

Creative Curiosity

Creative curiosity is the forerunner of creativity. To activate creativity in your child, encourage him to ask questions about everything and anything. Allow him to strike out and explore new experiences for himself. This way, he will get new ideas. For example, an author who has experienced life will be able to write a book that will be an amalgamation of all that he has seen and heard. He will be an even better writer if he has analysed events or understood human nature with all its strengths and weaknesses and paradoxes.

Keeping this in mind, always give your full attention when the child is asking questions. When we are young, we are taught to honour and respect our elders. It holds true the other way around too. As a child, how many of us would respect an adult who sneers, patronizes or even ignores us?

I remember an incident that occurred not too long ago. I was chatting with a neighbour who had dropped in with her son. The doorbell rang. I was pleasantly surprised to see an old friend. 'Am I disturbing you?' she asked. 'I've brought my daughter along too.'

'Of course not. Come in,' I said, invitingly.

The minutes slipped by. The two children got along like a house on fire. But I noticed something strange about my neighbour. From the time my friend had walked in, my neighbour ignored her and her daughter. All her remarks were addressed pointedly to me as though she and I were the only people in the room. I had never encountered such possessiveness from an acquaintance and was deeply embarrassed. My friend handled the situation

gracefully though I suspect she was a bit puzzled. However, her little four-year-old daughter was more frank. When her childish, friendly overtures were pointedly ignored by my neighbour, the little girl went off to play with the boy. Later, we heard her say rather loudly, 'You come to my house, but do not bring your mother!'

Though this little incident has no direct bearing on genius-making, I've recounted it to demonstrate how indifference puts off a child. So we must remember never to be indifferent. In fact, you must honour and respect the child's questions. Take time over answering his queries. Help him find the answers.

Expand his mind by raising additional questions. Make him consider new possibilities. For example, if you read aloud Red Riding Hood's story to him, after the reading session is over, hold a question-answer session.

'What are the things Red Riding Hood saw in the forest on the way to her grandmother's place? What kind of tree was the woodcutter cutting — an oak tree? Or a pine tree? And so on....

While out on a walk, you can bring various scenes to the child's notice. For example: 'Why are these men digging up the road? Why has the shopkeeper displayed that washing machine in the window? How does that fountain on the junction work? How is the water flowing into it?' Since there is almost always a colourful landscape around the fountain, you can discuss the colour combinations. 'Would purple have looked brighter instead of that pale lemon?'

The possibilities are endless. But then, so is the growth of a genius endless.

Inspired Imagination

In school, your child is taught facts about every subject — geography, history, biology, mathematics, civics, social studies. But facts without imagination are like photographs without colours (that includes black and white). I wish every school had a subject called *inspired imagination*. It would be a time where every child could dream up impossible-sounding, improbable inventions — for example, cats that can fly, or a land where children remain children all their lives....

Inspired imagination is the oxygen of creativity. It breathes life and colour into it and adds an element of fun to everything. It's a make-believe world that vibrates with energy. It may sound silly or fanciful, but it has a serious and very practical side too. For example, a scientist first imagines a certain situation. Then he works on facts towards it. If one experiment fails, he has to use his imagination to dream of another way to approach that situation. It's the same in all professions.

Your child could have his or her own problem. She may hate the thought of homework. But suppose she were to imagine that there was a Good Fairy hovering over her, helping her, talking to her, encouraging her ... the homework would turn into a fun-session with the Good Fairy sitting on her shoulder!

So never scoff at a child's imagination, however wild the story may sound. I've heard a father reacting angrily by shouting, 'What nonsense are you talking about? Who has been filling your mind with such rubbish?' His child could, either, become a *closet-imaginer* or worse still, not dare to imagine too much in future. For a genius, a mental prison is claustrophobic. Let him be free to conjure up stuff that only dreams are made of. Big ideas can, sometimes, stem from wild dreams. Let him dream big. It's the right of a genius.

Independence

After the first two stepping-stones, the third one should follow naturally. Independence is the elixir of a genius. If your child is hesitant or doubtful that he may be stepping out of a mould you have put him into, he will never be able to express himself creatively and, hence, will never make the grade of a genius. A genius needs to be secure that he won't face heavy disapproval. Then only will he allow himself to try something new. His success and satisfaction will stem from a willingness to try a new approach. In your love and your support lies his independence. Where would Leonardo da Vinci have been if he had not gone against certain norms? More important, where would we be?

Independence is a vital element. It builds up the child's confidence. Knowing that you will not disapprove spurs him on. Independence is a process in the continuous whirling wheel of creative mental growth. Only if the child is given space and the freedom to grow, will he flower into a genius.

The Stepping-Stones at Work

The three stepping-stones are vital for the creativity of a genius. I will give you a fitting example of genius at work through these three stepping-stones. I was at a grocer's shop when a mother and daughter walked in. The little one was about eight or nine years old. With her round bright eyes, she looked at everything in the shop. Occasionally she would ask her mother what something was. Sometimes she would pick up something to examine it. Her mother did not reprimand her but told her quietly to handle the object carefully and put it back in its original place after she was done with it. Creative curiosity and independence were very much in evidence there!

Then, there was a minor disturbance. The mother wanted to buy one kilogram of pulses. The shopkeeper could not find his weight-measure — that heavy piece of metal which is kept on one side of the scales to balance and determine the exact amount of the required object. He went on searching for some time, getting angrier and angrier with himself at making a customer wait. He even cuffed his helper — a young boy.

I was about to step in with a suggestion when the little girl piped up. 'Why don't you use that as a measure?' she told the shopkeeper. He turned to look at what she was pointing at. It was a carton of *Basmati* rice[1] with One Kilogram written across it! I was taken aback at the little girl's quick intelligence and also at the coincidence. I had been about to make the suggestion myself when she had spoken up! To come back to the point I was making, here was a classic case of the three stepping-stones at work. The little girl had already demonstrated her curious nature. She had let her imagination work through her observations. Secure in her confidence, she was independent enough to make a suggestion that proved to be really constructive!

To Conclude

By encouraging your child to cross the three stepping-stones, you are handing your child the strong sceptre of creativity. Creativity is the forefather of possibilities. Possibilities are the terrain of a genius. From one flows the others. Let the powerful current of creativity flow on in the genius!

---

[1] A kind of fine, fragrant rice.

11

Fine-Tuning a Genius

Education is not received; it is achieved.

Proverb

During one of my visits to a school, a little boy came up to me and said wistfully, 'You are lucky. I wish I were like you. I'd get all my math answers without having to work at them.' At first I was amused and then, a little concerned.

'Getting the right answer is only one part of it,' I told him. 'But it is as important to understand the method that gets you the right answer.'

I do not know if I got through to him, but he went away looking a little happier! I have cited this example because some parents feel that their child is a good student because he or she gets fairly good marks at school. They do not really see if the child enjoys or understands his studies. Some children simply memorise the contents of their books, and during exams, write parrot-like answers.

While a good memory is a blessing, by itself, it will take your child only so far and no farther. As responsible parents, you must realize that. A newspaper once quoted findings from a national poll: Two out of every three parents listed, admitted to lack of parental concern, attention and supervision.

If you belong to the two-out-of-every-three category, I would suggest that you galvanise yourself into taking positive action. If you want your child to be a genius, you must turn him into a superlearner. Just as a radio needs to be tuned to get the best reception, you will have to fine-tune your child's skills, attitudes and behaviour pattern before he can become a genius. For that, you will have to ensure that he imbibes the quality of being SUPER into his system — that is what will give him the edge over mediocrity.

Supermotivation

Supermotivation stems from independence. Somewhere in his mind, the child already knows that both parents and teachers are instrumental in his learning process. He turns to you and his teachers to get the right answers. But what he must realize is that while you can supply the required information, no one can do his learning for him. He has to do it himself. This is where independence comes in from an early age.

Recently, a friend of mine moved into a new neighbourhood. When I visited her in her new surroundings, I asked her, 'What are your neighbours like?'

'Good!' she replied unhesitatingly. 'Except for one thing.' 'What's that?' I asked.

'Once they came to know that I am a teacher, they started sending their children with all kinds of problems to me!' she laughed. Then she looked serious. 'You know what surprises me! Parents send their children expecting me to spoonfeed them. The other day, a little girl came over saying she wanted me to write an essay on dogs!'

'What did you do?' I asked interestedly:

'I gave her some books and asked her to read them. She was unwilling at first. But as I discussed them with her, she became interested and then, exuberantly enthusiastic! Then, she said: "You know what I like best about dogs! Their soft, friendly eyes and their friendly, wagging tails!" Then she added slowly and thoughtfully, "I wish I had a tail to wag." '

'I asked her why. She told me quite a tale.'

'Go on,' I encouraged my friend, deeply absorbed in her narration.

'She told me: "Last year, a sad little boy joined our class. My teacher told us that he had lost his father in the Iraq war and that we must be kind and helpful to him. I wanted to help him, but I didn't know how." '

'Then she looked at me with her big, soulful eyes and said, "If I had a tail, I'd have wagged it, so that he would have known that I wanted to be friends with him!" '

100

'She sounds like a lovely child!' I exclaimed. My friend looked at me smilingly.

'She does, doesn't she?' she agreed. 'But it gave me the opening I needed. I said, "You are a good-hearted child! Now, why don't you write about this incident in your essay?" '

'She looked at me half-eagerly, half-doubtingly.'

'Can I?' she asked.

'Of course,' I replied.

'And you know something! She sat down there and then wrote a beautiful essay! When she showed it to me, I said, "Excellent! Your parents and teacher will be very proud of you!" '

'And you're a wonderful teacher' I said quietly.

What had my teacher-friend done? She had spent a little time with the girl and motivated her. She had also made the little girl realize that only she could do her work herself. Later on, I heard from my friend that the little girl's essay had created quite a stir. She had got the highest marks in her class and was asked to read it out aloud to her fellow-students. It was an honour that boosted her confidence no end. After that, she wrote her essays all by herself, always scoring good marks. The girl wants to be a writer when she grows up!

So you can see how a little effort goes a long way! I'm a strong believer in supermotivation. I would liken my friend's effort to throwing a small pebble in still waters. That tiny splash created wider and wider ripples until the little girl even found her vocation and career!

To supermotivate your child, you must spend some time with him, understand him, guide him. Let him do his own work and take the responsibility for it. It is important that you acknowledge the fact that he spends time and effort on his studies and show your appreciation about it. For example, you can tell your spouse loud enough for your child to hear, 'Bunty is so independent and intelligent. Today, he wrote a beautiful essay on dogs all by himself.'

Your spouse can reply, 'Is that so? I must read it!'

Or when your child shows a good report card, you must congratulate him or her. Child psychologists call this the Earshotting Method.

Praise is music to a child's ears. You can reward him too. Treats or trips or an extra privilege go a long way towards supermotivation. Projected dreams are also extremely effective. If you tell the child how his hard work and intelligence will, one day, get him a prestigious scholarship and then, a fantastic job in the future, it will motivate him to work harder.

Superconcentration

I think one of the biggest disservices a teacher does to a child is when she writes the remark *'inattentive'* in the report card. The child takes the report card home. The parent exclaims in horror over that remark and reprimands the child: 'You must pay attention in class!'

In effect, what are the teacher and parents doing? They are jointly giving and reinforcing in the child, a negative self-image — that he is inattentive. Instead of doing that, I would advise the teacher to have a quiet word with the parents. They, in turn, should take subtle steps to correct this weakness and guide the child towards superconcentration.

The first step towards superconcentration is giving the child a positive image of himself. For example, if he finishes a jigsaw puzzle, you can praise him by saying, 'Excellent! Did you know that only a child with superconcentration can finish a jigsaw puzzle in such a short time? Quick! Go and tell Daddy!'

Your child, happy at the attention that he is getting, will go and report dutifully to his father. By now he is already telling himself that he has superconcentration. The father, of course, has to give a suitably appreciative reply too.

You can use various situations to reinforce this positive image. For example, if your child is a keen fan of cricket and his hero is Sachin Tendulkar, you can use the latter's example to teach a valuable lesson. Tell him, 'Sachin Tendulkar is a good cricketer because he has superconcentration. I am sure you have it too!'

Tell him that he should always say, 'I CAN DO IT!'

You can weave anecdotes about people who, when confronted with problems, would mutter four magic words to themselves: 'I can do it!' Then, they would call upon their superconcentration powers, and hey presto! They did it!

By blending positive self-imagery and anecdotes, you can, indeed, make your child develop superconcentration.

Superunderstanding

Here, I would like to start with a quote from *How Children Fail* by an American author-teacher, John Holt. Holt writes: 'By intelligence' we mean a style of life, a way of behaving in various situations. The true test of intelligence is not how much we know how to do, but how we behave when we don't know what to do.'

This is where superunderstanding comes in. It means applying skills to confront new, unknown situations. A genius is not just a powerhouse of information. So is an encyclopedia or a computer. A genius is one who can use this knowledge in a certain situation.

A child or an adult who has not cultivated super-understanding is sure to panic and give up when confronted with a new problem. To test this for yourself, try solving the problem given below. First try it on yourself and then on your child. Solve it mentally. Do not use paper and pen. Take exactly five minutes and no more. Calculators are not allowed. Here's the problem:

2xl0x25x6x4x3x32x0x5x22xllx4x3x45x3l652

What is the answer? An average person will take one look at the long series of numerals and give up, saying, 'I can't do it.'

How will a person who has cultivated superunderstanding tackle it? He will begin with the premise that nothing is too difficult; that sometimes the most complex of problems can be solved easily and simply. Five minutes is not as short a time as it seems. He will scan the numerals carefully. Within a minute, he will have the answer. The answer is zero!

Such a person has taken the trouble to spend a few seconds scanning the figures. When he sees the zero tucked in the middle, he will know he has to proceed no more. His knowledge will tell him that any number multiplied by zero is zero. He will have the answer on his fingertips!

Superunderstanding stems from the same source as super-concentration — the *I-can-do-it* philosophy. In fact, it goes one step further. A child who has superunderstanding knows that he has to look up his text books and reference books for answers. If, by chance, they do not contain the answers, he knows how to get help from other sources. He knows he can always ask you or his teachers. He begins on a superpedestal because he has already grasped and understood that nothing is impossible.

The Three-Pronged Strategy

To help the child develop superunderstanding, teach him the three-pronged strategy. Since most children are television-viewers, they are familiar with sophisticated-sounding words. You can make this strategy exciting and interesting by calling it Operation Destination. There are three steps to it:

1. Data
2. Method
3. Destination

Here is one example of how Operation Destination can be put to use. Consider this problem:

Bob is as old as Pat was five years ago. Jim, who is fifteen years old, is four years older than Pat. What age is Bob?

Now for Operation Destination:

Data: Bob is as old as Pat was five years ago.

Fifteen-year-old Jim is four years older than Pat.

Method: Pat's age = Jim's age − 4 = 15 − 4 = 11.

Therefore, Pat's age = 11.

Bob's age = Pat's age − 5.

Therefore, Bob's age = 11 − 5.

Destination: Bob's age is 6.

Explain Operation Destination to your child this way. Your child has to understand that there is a *destination* to be reached. The next step is to carefully follow the *data*. Then, use the *method* to reach the destination.

This is, of course, only one small example of super-understanding. But you can use similar ways and means to teach logic and understanding.

Supermemory

In Chapter 6, I had discussed how by storytelling you can open your child's inner-movie. Now you are in a position to build upon it. Super-remembering is the ability to hold and store images in the mind's eye. You can give your child the great gift of a supermemory by stimulating him with a lively discussion.

Given below is a scene from the *Mahabharata* where the teacher, Dronacharya, is teaching Prince Arjun how to shoot with a bow and arrow. The discussion on the picture can go this way:

Mother: 'What is Prince Arjun shooting at?'

Child: 'A bird.'

Mother: 'Where is the bird?'

Child: 'Up on a tree ... on one of the branches ... it's red in colour and stands out against the green leaves ... it's pretty high up ... I don't know how Prince Arjun can aim for only the eye....'

Mother: 'Has Prince Arjun angled his arrow right?'

Child: Well, yes, I think he has.... He must have because he does get it at the end. But here, if I draw a straight line ... (draws) ... I don't know....'

Mother: 'What is Prince Arjun wearing?'

Child: 'A red ... (hesitates) outfit? It's got a red belt drawn into a big bow ... he's got a crown on his head ... a bracelet on his arms ... that looks like a pearl necklace around his neck. He's got a quiver full of arrows strung on his back....'

Mother: 'How is he standing?'

Child: 'With his legs wide apart ... can't see his feet ... they are hidden by the grass ... it's long....'

Initially, you can show him pictures. Later, he can form his own pictures in his mind by reading a paragraph from a book. Such exercises will strengthen his ability to retain information.

If you can direct his great mental energies into these four channels of supermotivation, superconcentration, superunderstanding and supermemory, your child will definitely turn out to be a genius.

However, make sure that all these exercises are done in an informal, relaxed atmosphere. The child should never feel that he is on an eternal test. This will create stress within him which will be self-defeating. Anxiety is a negative force that should never be allowed to creep in.

Another important factor to be remembered is that he must be given opportunities. Outings, tinged with informal education, give him a feel of what he sees or reads about in books. They add depth to his knowledge. They allow him to talk from first-hand experiences. They also add to the fun in life, making it exciting, rewarding and supermotivating.

To Conclude

Geniuses are not those who merely possess a good memory. The extra special quality that sets them apart from ordinary youngsters is the desire to achieve; to accept nothing as impossible, and to persevere till success lies in their palms.

12

Your Genius Must Write

*Reading maketh a full man; conference, a ready man; and
writing, an exact man.*

Francis Bacon

Theere is magic in writing! When a child begins to write, he is
experiencing certain vibrations or fluttering in the brain brought
on by thinking. The next step is that he wants to communicate
those thoughts. You may say: 'But he can talk!' Yes, he can. But
he's already achieved that. That is the first stage.

The next stage is drawing. It is also a wonderful means of
communication. I remember a beautiful advertisement that
appeared on television years ago. It showed a child's hand drawing
stick figures with arms and legs. The first figure was drawn with
the child saying, 'That's my Daddy.' With the next one, he
said, 'That's my Mummy.' Then he drew a small stick figure.
He hesitated, then erased the legs and said, 'That's me.' The
advertisement was for the handicapped. It was one of the most
powerful, most moving commercials I have ever seen. Even now,
when I think of it, it evokes strong emotional feelings in me.

Drawing is a very important stage for a child. It communicates
his feelings at a simple level. It is the forerunner of writing. That
does not imply that it is a lesser form of writing. Far from it! It

is a great art in itself. But it has its limitations because it has not been developed into a science. Not everyone can understand the complex thought process that is painstakingly put down on a large canvas by an artist. It is a communion purely between the artist and his pen or brush.

However, that is not the case with writing. It is an art too. But it is a universal communicator. The fairly new journalist initially concentrates on the art part of it — using long, difficult words by referring to the Thesaurus. But as he matures, his writing style becomes simpler and he evolves into a better communicator.

The child-genius must be encouraged to draw. Let him have his own sketch-book and pencils. Let him draw to his heart's content. And as he talks, draws and learns to read, introduce him gradually to writing. You will find that an excessively talkative child will be at peace with himself when he writes.

Develop Your Child's Writing Skills

Writing will give him a sense of joy and satisfaction. It is exhilarating because it lets off steam. The privacy afforded by pencil and paper allows him to let himself go, to let his hair down. In a sense, writing is the same as word-drawing or word-painting. And it is a must in the development of a genius.

Unfortunately, it is impossible for a teacher to give individual attention to students. But as a parent, you must concentrate on this aspect. Writing develops clarity of thought, the ability to be coherent and a certain sense of discipline or organization. It makes the child a good communicator.

Take an Active Interest

Since your goal is to make writing easier, more lucid and, hence, more productive for your child don't force him. Show interest, encourage him with praise and make it an enjoyable pastime. Read stories and poems to him. The sheer music and rhythm in poetry will catch the child's imagination. Make sure you read blank verse too. Or the child will have the misconception that poetry is pure rhyming!

Play word-games like Scrabble. It's a family game with the spice of competition stirred into it. Let him refer to the dictionary. I remember participating in a game of Scrabble with a family. The youngest child formed the word Rumpy. Instantly, there was an indignant uproar from his older brother and sister. 'There's no such word!' they protested.

'There is' he insisted. To prove his point he brought out a huge giant of a dictionary and showed the word to them! Till today, I do not know if he bluffed and that, by sheer luck, the word was in the dictionary, or whether he already knew it!

You can also play family games with synonyms and antonyms. They can be both educative and exhilarating. Another game involves asking each member of the family to find words or phrases that read the same frontwards or backwards. We've all heard of Napolean's famous words: 'Able was I ere I saw Elba.' Read backwards, it says the same thing.

Such fun games add to the child's vocabulary and will help when he begins to write. Vocabulary-building is the key to genius development. Include crossword puzzles, anagrams and cryptograms designed for children.

Let Him Express His Thoughts in Writing

You may be a working parent who, try as you might, cannot spend enough time with your child. And here is the sparkling, bubbling, talkative youngster who wants to chatter nineteen to the dozen! Ask him to write down his thoughts. It's a good beginning for the budding genius.

Children also find it easier to write down something they are; for some reason they are unable to express themselves directly. A mother once showed me a little note written to her by her three-year-old daughter even though they both happened to be home at the same time! It read: 'My brother hit me!'

Also, the spoken word tends to be direct. For example, a child may exclaim, 'It's raining!' But ask him to write about it. He may come up with, 'It is raining. The rain looks like arrows coming down from the sky.'

Or, here's a poem written by a six-year-old. I've stuck faithfully to the spellings as written by the child.

The fish leap out of the pond in glee,
The frogs thrust up their head to see,
The ducks are as happy as ducks can be.
It's raining!

The grass is drinking long and deep,
The flowers wake up from their drowsy sleep,
Out of the earth, the earthworms creep,
It's raining!

The raindrops sink in the thirsty ground,
And hang from the dry leaves gistening round,
The world is full of gurgurling sound,
It's raining!

Don't Restrict Movement or Time

In the previous chapters, I have emphasised how important it is for the child to have his or her own den amply stocked with pencils and paper. But if he or she wants to write on the dining table during non-meal times, do not force him to go to his den. It should not feel like a punishment. Allow his creativity and his communication to flow wherever it pleases.

If you've asked your child to write down his thoughts, don't hover around him until he has done the needful. Give him time. He needs to think. Thinking is a very important process of writing. Famous authors have said that it is thinking that takes more time than the actual writing. So you may find your child dawdling by sharpening his pencil, reading or even staring out of the window. Leave him alone. He is dawdling creatively. He may be *thinking* his way to becoming a genius!

Show a Positive Response

Your response should be encouraging and always a *pick-me-up*, not a *put-downer*. *You* should be interested in what he writes, not how he writes. Minor errors, at this stage, are ignored by the wise parent. It is the ideas and putting them together that are important, not your child's spellings or grammar.

Never Write for Your Child

Never write an essay or anything that will be turned in as his work. Never rewrite his work. As important as the act of writing are other factors: meeting a writing deadline, and taking responsibility for the finished product. He must enjoy the glow of ownership for his work. It will build up his confidence and teach him independence as well as discipline.

Avoid Criticism

Every genius thrives on praise. Your approach must be positive. Always look for the good points and praise him. Pick out specific points for praise. Some of the factors to look for in a genius' works are: accuracy, vivid descriptions, thought-provoking and interesting ideas and imagination. Find them and praise him for his perception.

Allow Him to Imitate

Initially, your child may imitate a certain author whom he or she admires. Don't worry or point it out. Imitation is a good beginning. Soon you will find he is adapting the idea. For example, I know of a children's writer who, in her childhood, admired Enid Blyton's books. Her favourites were the Famous Five and the Five Find-outers series. Her first book was modelled on the Blyton style. It was called *The Thrilling Three!* Later, your child will find himself and become an *original* writer.

Encourage Correspondence

Your child needs to *feel-and feed* his writing. Encourage him to write letters to relatives or friends on occasions rather than resort to greeting cards with their ready-made quotations. I know of a child who makes her own cards and inscribes her own words in them. Often, a caring relative sends a delighted reply. That acts as a motivation for the child.

This is also a good time to encourage him or her to have a penfriend. Sending letters with photographs and little gifts is as invaluable an experience as receiving them. It is also akin to opening a window — through language — to the world outside.

Teach Him to Transcribe

If your child likes a particular song, encourage him to learn the words by transcribing them from the radio, stereo/tape player to paper. He can also write down words, phrases, favourite poems and quotations from books, plays and television programmes.

Let Him Make Lists

Making lists helps the child to develop an organised mind. Encourage him or her to make lists of his records, tapes and books. This way, he will have his own organised library. If you are setting out on a vacation, let him make a list of the clothes and accessories that the family is packing and carrying with it.

On a day he feels overwhelmed by the load of homework, encourage him to make a list. Then, as he finishes each subject, he will enjoy ticking it off and tackle the next one with a new verve!

Keeping a Journal

Journals or diaries provide excellent writing practice for the genius. They are good outlets and can be the child's best friends. *Anne Frank's Diary* was a bestseller amongst both adults and children. They shared her personal feelings — the pleasures, the disappointments, the perceptions. A friend of mine, who was only eight years old during the 1962 Indo-Chinese war, recently told me that *Anne Frank's Diary* had inspired her to keep her own diary. 'I even kept the melted portions of the wax from the candles we used during the black-outs!' she said. 'It helped me because it drove away my fear of the war and lent an aura of romance instead, to the whole scenario!'

While one would not wish a war situation on our children, the above example does illustrate the good effects of keeping a diary. It serves as a catharsis and sharpens perceptions.

Your child can maintain a weather log, a news journal or a travel journal. A news journal can be given a professional touch by cutting out relevant headlines from newspapers and sticking them on to it. A travel journal can contain pictures and postcards. This is a wonderful way to learn writing.

To Conclude

One day, your child could become a famous author or journalist. In fact, writing helps in any profession. An executive can get his project or idea through with clear, strong, persuasive and powerful writing. So, take note: your genius must write!

13

A Positive Self-Image

Confidence begets confidence.

Latin Proverb

What does your child see when he or she looks into the mirror? You will probably answer with some degree of surprise and, perhaps, impatience: 'Himself, of course! He'll see his own face, what else!'

But that is not what I am getting at. Let me put it this way. What does your child see when you place a huge slab of chocolate in front of him? No, don't give me the obvious answer. This is not one of those anti-climatic riddles. Describe the child's feelings when he views this big, rich, brown, gleaming block of confectionery. His reaction is most likely to be: 'Yummy! I'm going to eat it!'

Now place his least favourite food — perhaps, spinach — in front of him and view his reaction. He'll probably wrinkle his little nose and announce in disgust: 'Spinach ! Ugh!'

To elaborate on these two situations, I'd call the first reaction to the chocolate — a positive reaction, while the second one, which is obviously an opposite one, is a negative reaction.

To come back to my first point. What does your child feel when he sees his reflection? Is it a positive reaction or a negative one? You will probably be surprised at my question. 'I've never given it thought!' you may exclaim. Let me tell you what the child sees. True, his reflection shows him a normal enough face — more likely, a sweet, innocent face. But does he perceive it that way? What he perceives is the *self-image* he carries within him.

To give you an example: I saw a film entitled *Separate but Equal* starring Sidney Poitier. It is a powerful film depicting racism and the black people's fight for real equality with the whites. In the film, there is an extremely sensitively crafted scene. Little black children are given two dolls — a black one and a white one. They are asked which is prettier. Without hesitation, every black child picks out the white doll. I rocked in my chair as the implication hit me. What a terrible legacy to burden our children with! The black children's self-esteem and self-image was so low, almost non-existent. To them the white doll was pretty or superior. It brought home the terrible fact that not only were the blacks looked down upon by the whites, but even by themselves. With such a negative thought deeply embedded within themselves, how could black children rise even when given an opportunity?

So you realise the importance of my question when I ask: What does your child perceive when he looks into the mirror? Your child perceives what you have poured into him: your reactions, your attitude, your body-language — all act as his pointers. Use strengths to overcome weaknesses. If you genuinely see your child as an achiever, and let him know that, he will see himself as an achiever. And achievement is the calling of a genius.

I know a woman who is not highly educated. She has not read books on bringing up children. Throughout her life, she has operated on instinct and her great love for her children. Every one of them is an achiever with plenty of self-confidence stacked inside him or her. How did she do it? Instinctively, she knew that her children looked to her for everything. So she was parent, teacher, artist, scientist, psychologist, child guide, student, judge, catalyst … as the occasion demanded. And along with that, her growing children were also secure in the fact that their mother loved them.

Her attitude, her reactions were purely out of instinct. If a child did particularly well in a subject, she would praise him for it. She would gently point out that with a brain like his, he could do equally well in other subjects too. Her attitude made the child think for himself, and made him work harder for it.

Today, she is all of seventy-plus. Even though her children have grown up, married and have their own children, she has the same attitude towards their new lives which involve career, marriage and children. Though she has done this without any deliberate effect, she has always capitalised on their strong points and used them to build up their weaker areas. Her daughter narrated an incident to me:

'My father always expected us to get full marks in Maths — a hundred on hundred — so we worked hard at it. One day, when I was in the second standard, I brought home a report card that surprised my parents. I had got full marks in Maths. But I had got 99 on 100 in History! My mother, I feel, realised that my father's goading had resulted in my obtaining full marks in Maths, and she saw that the same technique could be successful for other subjects too. After that, she encouraged me equally in all subjects instead of only in Maths!'

It is opportunities like these that should be seized by parents.

Promote Your Child's Interests

Too often, parents impose their one-dimensional view on their children. And by doing this, they snatch away the genius-element that was within reach.

The one-dimensional view has a selfish motive behind it. Very often, the father pushes the child towards developing a potential for the profession that he, the father, belongs to. If the father is an engineer, he wants the child to be one too. The emphasis is then purely on Maths. If the father is a businessman, he wants the child to follow in his footsteps. So the child is made to take up Business Management even though his interests may lie elsewhere.

Some parents are the other extreme. A doctor leading a hectic life, always being at the beck and call of his patients, may announce loudly: 'I'll never allow my son to be a doctor!' He will expect his friends to pat him on his back and say, 'You're a rare father not wanting your son to follow your profession!' But to my mind, both attitudes are wrong. The child should be allowed to formulate his own mind, chart his own life. Putting such thoughts into a child's head, and pushing the child towards or away from something, are equally limiting. If a person has a heavy stone tied to him and then he is put into a pond, what will his options be?

The only way he can go is down. You cannot tie your child down by your attitudes or your ideas. If his interests or inclinations lie in a different direction, you must give him leeway, the space to grow and flourish in his own area of interest.

Motivate Your Child

How must you view your child if you want him or her to be an achiever? First, you must realise that it is your responsibility to give your budding genius a strong, positive self-image. I've said right from the beginning of this book that every child is born a potential genius. You must believe it of your child, and not just discuss it as a general topic of interest at a cocktail party. If you believe genuinely that your child is a special individual, and allow your sincerity to show in your attitude, your child too will believe it. Your child will have a strong, positive image of himself and will work hard. The result? — An achiever! A genius!

What does a sculptor do? He takes the raw material — a block of wood or a lump of clay. He shapes it into a beautiful figure. How does he do this? He has seen the potential, believed in it and worked on it.

Not for a moment am I suggesting that your child's brain is a block of wood or a lump of clay. In fact, you are more privileged. Your child already has a beautiful gift from God — a marvellous brain with millions of folds of intelligence in it. All you have to do is enhance it.

It is your attitude that is the raw material. It is on your attitude that the child constructs his self-image. If you think he is an achiever, he will believe he has the qualities required to be an achiever. From your positive attitude will spring his positive attitude. Only from such an attitude are born confidence, optimism and the willingness to try.

Many parents and teachers make one big mistake. They think that if the child proves he is an achiever, he is one. If he doesn't, he proves that he is not. In other words, the ball is always in the child's court while the adult sits on judgement. So their attitudes are seen as a result rather than the cause of the child's success or failure. Such parents or teachers are viewing the child from the wrong end of the telescope. If you want your child to be an achiever, you must rid yourself of your negative or one-dimensional view.

Many parents may react with bewilderment and indignation. 'I've given my child every opportunity that is possible,' they'll say. 'I've given him books, toys, games, — what more can I do?' I'll answer that at length with some of my own questions. What has your attitude, your body language been when you gave your child these facilities? Have you taken an honest interest in your child's activities? I emphasise the word *honest*. You may have shown interest, encouraged him, supported him. But have they been honest efforts, backed by your strong belief in your child's extraordinary capabilities?

The child is extremely sensitive to the slightest of nuances in your tone, expression and body language. A forced, hearty word of encouragement, an over-bright smile, the curve of your body — these are the real monitors of your attitude towards your child. He can distinguish false praise from sincere appreciation, however subtle. A flicker of the eye speaks volumes to him.

Reach Out

If you believe that your child is an achiever, he will feel and act like one. I call this the *believe* and *feel-and-act* concept. Each parent should take a vow to follow the eleven commandments as follows:

I believe sincerely that my child is:

- extremely intelligent
- an achiever
- quick on the uptake
- a genius at studies
- excellent at sports
- very independent and hard-working
- helpful and obedient
- friendly and kind
- very popular with everybody
- very good-looking
- happy and brings happiness wherever he goes.

If you, as parents, hold on to these eleven commandments all the time and believe in them; if you show by your attitude that you are sincere about your belief; your child too will feel and act like an achiever.

To make you understand the intrinsic value of what I am advocating, let me expand a little more on this topic. Your child has an exemplary image — an ideal prototype — of who he passionately wants to be. This comprises of those qualities that he knows you, the parent, admire and applaud. By your encouraging, honest and loving attitude, he will strive to fit the exemplary image. In doing so, he will enjoy the glow of well-being, together with the success and admiration it will bring him. And the exemplary image will become his real self-image. The achiever will be born! The genius will be made!

Love Will Show The Way

I always emphasise the loving attitude because it waters down the impossibly high standards of expectations from a parent. High expectations can also work against the achieving attitude. If a child cannot meet your high standards, he becomes anxious. He is so worried that he cannot give his best. His performance drops. Since he cannot live with this feeling of failure, he reacts like any child would in these circumstances. His exemplary image takes a blow. It is no more the self-image he was striving for. He perceives himself as one who is not capable. With this shatteringly negative outlook, he becomes slack in his work and deliberately turns in poor work.

Paradoxically, he feels he has achieved what he is capable of achieving. Scoldings and punishments only prove his 'achievements' of being a non-achiever. To other children in the same boat, he is a hero. School and lessons become a drag. So he continues to be a deliberate non-achiever to achieve and maintain the status of a hero!

On the other hand, if you have poured in positive inputs and, simultaneously, not set impossibly high standards, the child works freely and without stress towards turning the exemplary image into the real self-image, and becomes a true achiever!

To Conclude

Your child's achieving attitude begins with you. If he senses that you strongly and sincerely believe that he has that extra-special quality in him, he will rise to it naturally. With self-worth and self-confidence working their powerfully potent magic in him, he will become a true achiever — a great genius!

14

From Ordinary to Extraordinary

Genius is one per cent inspiration and ninety-nine per cent
perspiration.

Thomas Alva Edison

Floods, earthquakes, typhoons and all kinds of disasters may hit
the world. But what keeps the human race going? It is a powerful
force within us, an eternal spring of energy called motivation.
I think that that is what Noah's ark represents in the Bible —
motivation. Lord Krishna's wise philosophy promulgates the same
motivation. Saints and scientists alike have illumined the world
with their findings — the result of their deep motivation.

It was Lord Buddha's motivation that drove him to give up
his princely life in search of *nirvana*[1] and give the world a new
religion.

It was Thomas A. Edison's motivation that snuffed out ten
thousand failures and, finally, switched on the incandescent electric
light to beam the great electrical age into our lives and homes.

It was Mahatma Gandhi's motivation that sent the British
government and army out of India, giving the great country its
freedom.

---

[1] Salvation.

At an individual level, it is positive motivation that elevates us from the ordinary to the extraordinary. It is this powerful force that makes us believe in our potential and disbelieve our doubts. If you want your child to be a genius, you must inject in him this great force — this propelling power of positive motivation.

The greatest news that I can give you is that your child is born with *natural motivation.* It is circumstances that pull us down and swamp us with the twentieth century disease — depression. But it is a disease seen only in adults or in children who may have come across man-made ills too early in life.

Six Motivating Mantras

To enhance your child's natural motivation, let your attitude and environment be permeated by these six motivating *mantras:*

1. Provide an exciting, healthy, learning atmosphere in the house.
2. Keep your own and your child's mind always busily engaged and occupied with positive objectives.
3. Always associate yourself and your child with people who breathe and inspire positive motivation and action. Refuse to be influenced by the *put-downers* or negative thinkers.
4. Positive auto-suggestions or self-talk are also powerful forces that propel motivation.
5. Never colonialise your child's brain. Always encourage his creative independence.
6. Introduce him to the world of great men and women — inventors, sages, statesmen....

Do You React Negatively?

So far, I have spoken about an entity called *parent.* Now, I'd like you to examine the individual roles of a mother and a father.

Though I realize that with working mothers increasing in number, there is sure to be a blending of roles, yet, their individual roles are singularly important.

If a child is highly motivated, both parents can share the credit equally. Obviously both have worked positively towards encouraging the child. But if you find your child holding back in some ways, examine yourselves. Where have you gone wrong?

Mother: Do you react in a neutral manner to your child's accomplishments?

Do you punish him for his failures?

Father: Are you remote and not involved in your child's upbringing?

Do you insist and demand a high standard of excellence in performance?

As you can see, in both cases, there are negative reactions that will lower the child's motivation. Indifference and non-involvement equal negativity. Punishments and excessive demands push the child into a corner. A child needs your positive involvement, encouragement, praise and reward.

You want your child to lead an exciting life full of purpose, full of accomplishments, full of happiness. In short, you want your child to lead a life of fulfilled genius. So where do you find the motivation that is required in a genius? The answer is: *everywhere.*

From the Ordinary to the Extraordinary

As you read each chapter, you may feel that too much is expected from you. But pause for a moment and think. Are you expected to go out of your way? On the contrary, you will find yourself a happier person if you contribute positively to your child's development. You too will be learning and growing in the process.

So with a clear mind and positive thoughts, let us set off to create our own list of dos and don'ts that will elicit the best from the child.

Allow Individuality to Blossom

Free your child from a mental prison. Encourage the free flow of independent thoughts and actions from an early age. Your home should be like a huge highway where the traffic flows freely without any signals except at critical junctions. Too many *don'ts* will restrict the genius in your child. Let him be. For the genius, the world is there to be conquered, not to be observed with fear.

Learning by Doing

Let your child do things for himself. He may fumble and stumble, but that is a process of learning. Curb your desire for *instant perfection.* Even instant coffee has to dissolve before you can drink it. To give you an example: Leta wanted to learn cooking when she was about twelve years old. Her mother was a chef *par excellence.* Everybody praised her culinary efforts. So little Leta decided that she would ask her mother to teach her cooking. They entered the kitchen. But one hour later, Leta threw off her apron and walked out in a huff, vowing that she did not want to touch a gas stove as long as she lived. Why? Her mother insisted on Leta doing everything her way. The onions had to be chopped exactly to a given size and shape; the beetroot had to be sliced exactly to a certain thickness, and so on. The constant nit-picking took the joy out of cooking.

On the other hand, had her mother left her to potter around by herself after giving the basic instructions, the result may not have been an aesthetic delight; but the sparkle of satisfaction in Leta's eyes as her mother praised her would have sufficed. And the little girl would have been motivated to go on.

Don't Count Mistakes as Failures

There is no such thing as failure in life. Yet a child can be devastated when he or she makes a mistake. The mistake is not important in itself. It is not going to turn the world upside down. It is not going to suck the oxygen out of the air you breathe in, so why make such a big deal out of it?

Your response to a child's mistake should be neutral. Don't be disappointed because there is nothing to be disappointed about. There's a positive side to making mistakes. Tell your child that next time, he will do it right. Sometimes a mistake can even lead to a new discovery. For example, a scientist may put a wrong chemical in his mixture. But, voila! what comes out could be a great new discovery! So, remember, never reprimand or punish the child for failure.

Let Your Child Remedy His Own Mistakes

When a child first starts writing with a fountain pen, he may blot his homework. Relax! Don't chide him. You may have done the same yourself at his age. You can show him gently how to use blotting paper, and how he should hold the pen to obtain the best results. Your calm reaction will prove to him that there is always a solution.

The next time, he may have blotches on his book again. But remember, he is still motivated. He still wants to do it right. He has to find a way to do it right. Perhaps he will practise on a rough book before he writes it out neatly. The main point here is that *he is doing his work.* He is doing it even if he is doing it badly. Let him discover his own limitations and work around them. Don't set limitations and boundaries. You want a genius, not a robot!

Avoid Undue Interference

In learning to be independent, the child may do things that you find stupid and extremely objectionable. Leave him be. By interfering at this stage, you will only curb his independence. And that, in turn, will limit his mental growth.

Don't Force Your Ambitions on Your Child

Remember that your child is an individual — a thinking person with his own mind. Don't look upon him to fulfil your frustrated ambitions. In your youth, you may have wanted to be an artist, but financial circumstances may have forced you to take up a full-time job. But only you can fulfil your own ambitions even today. Don't force your dreams on your child. Let him create and fulfil his own dreams. He may want to become an artist. But that dream should spring from within him, not from your ambitions.

Set Reachable Goals

All of us need goals or a certain end in view — a certain destination. It helps us to focus and work towards a final result. It motivates us. I know a famous author who once confided in me that only when he received a deadline from his publisher, could he write the required number of words per day! Otherwise, he would feel he was working in a vacuum and not get on with the job!

Keeping this in mind, remember that inspiration and motivation arise from a set goal for your child. But before you get on with this important task, find out:

- Does your child want that goal? There's no point in forcing him to read, when he wants to write. First, satisfy yourself that your child wants what you want for him.

- Does your child believe he can reach the goal? If he does, go on. If he doesn't, don't push him into it by false assurances. Here, either change your track or go on to the next point.

- Set reachable goals. A step-by-step approach will pay great dividends. As the claim succeeds at one level, he will be motivated to try for a higher one. Remember, everything is possible, but it needs your gentle guidance and cooperation to make it work.

The reachable-goal practice is invaluable. It works with adults too. I know a lady who achieved success through this practice. She was a colossus of a woman in purely physical terms. Feeling breathless and weak, she went to the doctor. He examined her thoroughly and handed over his prescription.

'How often should I take it, Doctor?' she asked, putting the piece of paper carefully into her purse.

'As often as you can,' he replied.

He patted her saying, 'I know you will get well soon. But follow my prescription faithfully.'

'Yes, Doctor,' she said gratefully and rushed to the chemist. The chemist was obviously a wise, experienced man. He looked at the paper and told her, 'You are lucky. This is the most inexpensive medicine I've ever seen prescribed. You can do it at home for free. Why do you want to buy it?'

She took back the prescription with a puzzled look and read it. It said: Diet and exercise every day until you shed 30 kilograms!

When she reached home, she tacked on to her refrigerator door — the words 30 KILGRAMS, and began a rigorous dieting and exercising regime. Within two days, she was disheartened. 'Thirty kilograms!' she told herself. 'I'll never be able to do it!'

Then she was struck with an idea. 'I can do it,' she thought exultantly, 'if I do it right!' Carefully, she made a chart which set reachable goals. She would try to lose 2 kilograms in one month first. She stuck the chart on the refrigerator door and went to work on herself with renewed will.

Every month, she'd tick off the weight she had lost. It gave her a feeling of accomplishment and strong desire and motivation to

go on. When I met her, she had already lost 15 kilograms and her enthusiasm was undiminished. 'I'm going to lose those 30 kilograms!' she vowed. 'And maybe more after that!' She had *set* herself reachable goals and was finding this process both enjoyable and effective. Not only did the larger goal seem closer, she was now willing to look beyond it!

Similarly, you too can make a chart of reachable goals for your child. It will motivate him as he sees the tangible Tick against each step that he has mastered.

Encourage All-Round Development

A genius, as I've said earlier, is an all-rounder. He is not an armchair citizen. To be able to read or write independently is not the be-all and end-all of becoming a genius. A child needs to be patted or praised in other activities too. For example, send him out to purchase household goods. It is part of independence training. Or if he wants to earn his own pocket money, encourage him. It is part of his mental growth. Also, you are preparing your genius for a greater life. David Lewis, a psychologist, recommends encouragement to undertake some household duties for boys just as much as girls, and to assume responsibility for certain domestic chores. He explains: 'Research has established that such tasks are associated with an optimum need for achievement.'

To Conclude

I have outlined all the aspects required to motivate your child. But remember — it is always a balancing act. Your child should never be excessively motivated. Over-motivation results in impatience and frustration, or an aggressively competitive streak. What you must aim for is a motivated, happy, balanced genius.

15

Fostering Superlearning

Thinking without learning makes one flighty, and learning without thinking is disaster.

Confucius

Look around you. Gaze at the faces of various people of varied ages from different walks of life.

You will know a superlearner from the bright, lively eyes, the spring in the step, the ring in the voice. The superlearner is the person who is a student right through life: always eager to learn, bubbling with ideas, bursting with enthusiasm.

I know an 85-year-old man who is a superlearner. He has his own little business. He has travelled all over the world. 'The only place I haven't been to and plan to visit this year is China,' he told me. 'I want to go there before I grow old.'

The man reads five newspapers a day, follows the daily news bulletins on television closely, writes letters, rings up friends, goes for picnics, visits art galleries, attends seminars, writes articles.... His latest hobby is studying homeopathy. 'There's no end to learning,' he told me.

I think that in those five words he has captured the essence of superlearning. Not only does it connote a superior mode of learning, but by its high quality, ensures its longevity in the person.

If you turn your child into a superlearner from an early age, you will have given him a lasting gift that can never be tarnished with time. Superlearning, by its very nature, also enables your child to think big, have boundless enthusiasm and the *go-for-it* attitude. Superlearning, indeed, is the genius' birthright.

Imagine that you are sitting atop a cloud. A star-studded sky is spread above you. If you reach out, you can touch those twinkling balls of brilliance. That is superlearning — a sky scattered with shining nuggets of knowledge. Now pluck each one for your child. Open your palm and see what each star contains to make your child's life a glowing galaxy of superlearning.

The Three R's

What do we have here? Something that rolls off your tongue as easy as pie! The three R's — they stand for:

- Read and research
- Reinforce and reward
- Review and reapply

Read and Research

An excellent way to put this first 'R' into practice is to base it on national holidays. In India, it can be Mahatma Gandhi's birthday. In the USA, it can be Thanksgiving Day, and so on. The child looks forward to this holiday. You can add meaning to his excitement by encouraging him to read about Mahatma Gandhi and how he freed India from the shackles of British rule, or about the early settlers in the USA and their relationship with native Americans. Make it an enjoyable experience with a rousing discussion that is bound to stimulate the child's critical thinking. Let him ponder over why Mahatma Gandhi believed in non-violence, or why survival was so difficult during the early days of the Pilgrim settlement in the USA.

Reinforce and Reward

Apply the knowledge accumulated to everyday life. Mahatma Gandhi believed in the upliftment of the poor. Perhaps your child can feed some poor children. Or prepare traditional Thanksgiving dishes with your child helping you. The feeling of well-being is a reward in itself.

Review and Reapply

Over dinner, ask your child to list the ingredients and measurements used in preparing the special Thanksgiving meal. Ask questions like, 'Were all these items available to the early pilgrims?' Or you can narrate a tale on Mahatma Gandhi, and then, challenge your child to think by asking a question like, 'Would the great man have approved of the nation taking a holiday on his birthday?'

Reinforcing Superlearning

There are other ways too of fostering superlearning. A little imagination, and planning are all it takes!

Developing an Identity

Take a happy day in the life of your child — his birthday! Introduce him to great people who were born on the same day by letting him read about them. The magic world of the genius will thus open out to him, giving him a wonderful sense of identity.

Having Fun with Word-Games

Have fun with words! Make up tongue-twisters, alliterative sentences and rhymes. Have you tried, 'She sells sea-shells on the seashore' to be said at top speed? Make your child say it three times without faltering! You will have a rollicking time.

Play the Family Word-Game. It involves taking each alphabet of the name of each member and making new words with those alphabets. For example, take Angelina. What are the words that you can make from it? — An angel, line, nail, gain and so on.

Becoming a Newsreader

Tell your child that he's a news producer-cum-reader. Clip stories from the paper; watch news on television; pick up neighbourhood happenings. Now let him organise the material and read it out to you and the family. Help him with his grammar. He can even take a commercial break, where he can mime an advertisement to the accompanying music.

Compiling a Family Directory

If your child's name is Natasha, start the Natasha Telephone Exchange. Let her compile the Family Directory by arranging neatly, in alphabetical order, the names, telephone numbers and addresses of family friends. It has a nice ring to it, doesn't it?

Browsing in the Library

Your child will love being a member of the local library. He can have his own card or a page in the library register with his name at its head. Teach him how to use the reference system. Let him choose his own books. He'll love it!

Going on Nature Walks

Go for slow rambles or nature walks. Let your child describe what he or she sees, for example, the long, lazy, tree-lined avenue.... Can he hear the husha-husha rustle of the leaves? Or, mmm! ... smell the gummy fragrance of the bark?

Asking Questions

When your child has a reading assignment or has to listen to presentations in class, how should he do it? Most children would do just that much — read or listen. But the superlearner should have a two-step strategy:

Think about the topic

and

Make up questions

For example, if the topic is World War II, let your child mull over anything he knows about the war. Then he should frame questions such as: What caused the war? Was it necessary? What were the major events that took place? How did the war change the way people lived? What were the national boundaries before and after the war? What weapons were in use?

What makes a superlearner stand head and shoulders above the rest is his interest. A topic for study is not a mere assignment to be done and finished with. He uses this opportunity to learn more about the topic, understand it, focus on it, analyse it. This approach also facilitates superunderstanding. And since his own inputs are tremendous, he is going to remember whatever he has learnt vividly, assimilating it into the realms of his supermemory.

Making Inferences

Most parents and children are content to cruise along — passengers in the boat of education. Not so a superlearner! He explores the boat fully and even wants to see what lies beyond it. The superlearner is not just a passenger; he is a swimmer, a deep-sea diver, a fisherman. For example, if the child is reading about legendary police dogs who can sniff and track down a criminal, he can question what it is that dogs have that enables them to distinguish between human smells? His immediate thought after this can be: That means that each human smell is different from the another. Each human has a unique smell of his own. Is there a way of computing those smells like fingerprints? On the other hand, will a pair of twins have the same smell?

Or, if he reads about a new invention, let him ponder over how it would change people's lives and habits.

In school, he will study the circulatory system of the human body. Let him think about the maintenance or the wear and tear of this system. How do diet, exercise and illness affect it?

In effect, what is your child doing? He is not a passive sponge who is merely absorbing all the knowledge poured into him. He is absorbing it as reported, trying to make inferences and draw conclusions about it, and making it more meaningful. As a result, it sinks into his brain. The next time he hears something connected with it, he will instantly recall what he has already absorbed and will, therefore, understand it better than another child, who may have merely memorised the matter studied earlier and will later forget about it.

Put Your Child on the Right Track

How can you help to put your child on the track of superlearning? The strategy involves five interlinked steps:

Instant Inferences

Most children take the telephone for granted. So when they learn about the invention of the telephone, they are not really impressed. They do not appreciate the change it has brought about in the world. To the superlearner, however, such things should be explained through discussions. Let him consider a world without a telephone. What has the telephone done for us? If there were no telephones, what would we do — resort only to sending letters and visiting people? How would that affect our lives?

Building Bridges

The superlearner should build a bridge between new information and old. He should look for similarities and for improvements. He should also apply new knowledge to what he is already familiar with. A case in point would be the new video telephone vis-a-vis the ordinary one. Or, if he is studying the system of justice, he could relate the judge's role in settling disputes to his own experiences with arguments and disagreements.

Finding the Main Idea

When an apple is cut, a core is found inside. Similarly, when your child is learning or reading about something, he should constantly look for the core of the subject. What is the main idea? Take the telephone — what lies at the centre of it? Instant communication of course, and so on. Knowing the main idea adds to his understanding and keeps him actively engaged in studying.

Categorising Information

For your child, it is often a bewildering experience to learn and remember large amounts of varied information. He ends up desperately memorizing it and praying that he can recall it when required. There is no need for the superlearner to do this. Let him group the information into categories. For example, if he takes music classes, initially, he need not try to remember the names and characteristics of every single musical instrument. Instead, let him group them: percussion, woodwinds, strings and brass. He should do the same thing with other subjects too. Categorizing brings an orderliness to the mountain of information that is poured out every day. And by making tiny molehills of information, he can both understand and remember each category. This way, he automatically builds up the larger picture of the mountain too.

Creating Analogies

This implies connecting new, unfamiliar information with existing knowledge. I consider this to be the fun part of superlearning. Good writers, I've noticed, often use analogies to explain a new event or a new thought process.

For example, if the child is trying to learn the difference between arteries and veins ... arteries are thick and carry oxygen-rich blood from the heart ... they are like rich merchants loaded with diamonds from the king — the heart — and gallop away on their horses. Veins are relatively thin and carry oxygen-poor blood to the heart ... they are like poor people, carrying their small bundle of belongings to the king.

Analogies can be very imaginative, and their fun element helps the child absorb information which could otherwise sound dull and pedantic, and, therefore, boring.

Encourage the child to create his own analogies. He will love the process because it involves learning through story-telling. And therein lies the tale of the superlearner!

Setting Specific Goals

I have already discussed the benefits of setting reachable goals in Chapter 14. Refresh your memory by re-reading the chapter before you take it on from here.

In brief, I've suggested that if the final goal has to be reached, set up sub-goals. Depending on the subject, you can make a chart and call it Rashid's Geography Travelogue or Rashid's History Travelogue. The traveller, Rashid, (your child), stops at each station before he goes on to the next one and the next one, until he reaches the final destination. The broad outline of the chart can remain the same while the topics can differ according to the subject.

This method will add to his enjoyment as well as yours. For example, if he finds a chapter particularly difficult, he can come to you, the ticket-collector, and tell you, 'Mr T.C., I want to remove something from my suitcase, but the zipper is stuck! Can you help me, please?'

You can help him unzip the bag by explaining the chapter to him. As he masters each chapter, you can give him a ticket for the next station. When he's collected a specific number of tickets, you can give him a special treat, or an outing, or the special privilege of staying up one hour more than usual, and so on.

Widening His Knowledge

The more knowledge your child acquires at home, the greater will his chances be of becoming a superlearner. Take him on outings ... hold discussions ... ask questions ... in short, talk of anything and everything under the sun!

Recalling Experiences

Encourage your child to talk about an experience or event that you did not participate in or were not present at, such as a school picnic. This will give your child a chance to use his memory, reflect on his experiences, learn to describe people and events, and tell complete stories.

Making a Scrapbook

Whatever the age, a scrapbook is a must for the superlearner. The pre-schooler can cut pictures from magazines of items beginning with A — apple, airplane, automobile.... The next day, he can go on to B, then C, and so on.

The student can keep a scrapbook on a hobby, a favourite singer, sport, writer....

One woman reflected on how her mother had taught her the concept of *three-dimensional* through a scrapbook. 'She made me cut three-dimensional pictures from advertisements. I remember cutting out a camera ... my favourite was a cottage which had colourful gems on its roof!'

Yes, indeed, advertisements in magazines are full of such three-dimensional pictures!

To Conclude

Superlearning, as you may have concluded, is a wonderful art that gives your child every opportunity to learn and grow into a genius. This technique is unique because it never stales. Many children who are proclaimed geniuses in their early years suddenly burn out when they reach the competitive classrooms of school. But a superlearner never wears out because, to him, every step of life is a process of joyful learning and absorbing. It is an immortal flame that never burns out — like a star. Let your child reach for those stars of knowledge, of superlearning. Let your child's genius shine!

16

Developing a Supermemory

Method is the mother of memory.

Thomas Fuller

An incriminating object has been found at the Scene of a crime — say, a handkerchief. The police dog is made to take a good long sniff at it. Then it is let loose on the line-up of suspects standing in cubicles. The dog sniffs at each, and then, finally, zeroes in to the one who matches the smell of the handkerchief and wags his tail, barking happily, as if to say, 'This is the guy!

In the same line-up, the victim is called for a visual identification of the criminal. She looks at each face, studies it and ... 'I'm not sure,' she says helplessly. Oh, oh! her memory has let her down! Yet there have been cases where the victim has pointed angrily at the suspect, saying, 'He's the one!' Or, even in situations where the criminal has got away, the police-artist has been able to sketch, pretty accurately, the face based on the victim's description.

Comparing the *sniff-method* of the dog to the *sight-method* of the human, I am sure that we all wish our memories were as accurate as the dog's nose! How often we hear the phrase, 'I can never remember faces!' Or we have variations such as, 'I can't remember names, but I never forget faces.' How casually we treat

144

our memory and take it for granted! If we meet an actor we feel: 'He must be having a terrific memory to be able to learn all his dialogues!'

A Bad Memory: A Fallacy

The first realisation that we have to accept is that we all have terrific memories, except that we have not learnt how to use them! In fact, if a child, after burning the midnight oil and cramming for an exam the following day, ends up giving in a poorly answered paper, adults have a comfortable excuse for it: a bad memory. The child, thankful to have a way out, in that he cannot be blamed for something that is perceived as beyond his control, seizes gratefully on the same *bad-memory* excuse for his future shortcomings.

So, here we are, all of us, constantly assuring one another how poor we are at remembering; how we have no head for figures;

how we cannot remember what we had for breakfast that very morning ... it's not even seen as a slip-up, but a very natural state of affairs. Memory is only for the 'whiz-kids' — those smart, sharp young people and a few other ethereal beings that inhabit this planet earth!

I remember an incident that occurred years ago. It came to light that a minister in the government had not paid his taxes for some years. When asked why he had committed this offence, he replied without a blink, 'I forgot!'

I have mentioned this instance only to point out the ridiculousness of this *I can't-remember business.*

Your child needs a good memory to pass his exams with high marks. We may moan at our educational system and comment that it is a pity that our children have to rely so much on their memory; that they have to learn by heart rather than understand their Subject. We may discuss how the entire system needs a total revamping. But at the end of it all, reality stares us in the face: our children must improve their ability to remember to get a high percentage. Of course, this is only one part of genius-making. But we just cannot ignore it.

For example, your child may be able to work out a maths problem with brilliant accuracy and pass the examination with flying colours. But, on the other hand, if he cannot remember in which year the first man landed on the moon, or when World War II ended, or if he is unable to name the capital of Australia, his report will plunge downwards.

A good memory is important because it helps to apply thinking and intelligence to the ever-new supply of information. What most of us have yet to realize is that we are all born with equal powers in our brain. If I were to tell you that there is no such thing as a bad memory, you will probably hold yourself up as an example to prove this fallacy. But what I say is backed by psychologists who have researched and made an intensive study of the memory phenomenon.

The Brain: A Storehouse of Information

Our marvel of a brain is, amongst other things, a museum of microfilms. One of its most stricking features is its back-up system. In those minute grey folds, tons of information gets stored, which is why a tiny jolt of electricity can make you *see* a scene from your childhood, or a wafting fragrance can *recall* some other memory.

So, you see, a supermemory or a microfilm of a memory is already there within you or your child. What you have to do is to train it so that you can tap it whenever you need it.

For starters, I would suggest that you don't put it in your child's head that he has a poor memory. He does not. If he seems to have forgotten something, do not ask rhetorical questions like, 'Don't you remember?' or 'Have you already forgotten?' It reinforces within him, a false assumption that he has a poor memory. Instead, use more positive phrases like, 'Of course, you remember! Think back....'

The memory-part of the brain can be likened to a bedsheet on a drying line with clothes pegs. If you use only one peg for a wide bedsheet, the sheet will not hang properly and will not dry. But if you use the right number of pegs, you will get the desired result.

Apply this analogy to your child's memory. If you tell your child, 'Repeat after me — CONSTANTINOPLE' — he may get stuck and be unable to say it because the pegs in his brain may have been unable to catch it. But if you break the word down to its phonetic units — CON-STAN-TI-NO-PLE — and say it slowly and clearly, his brain will seize each syllable and commit it to memory. This is because each peg has held on to each sound unit and stored it.

It is not that a person with a good memory has the fast-forward ability of a tape deck to record a big single word at one go. Such a person, without realizing it consciously, has automatically broken down the word to its basic units and stored it away as CON-STAN-TI-NO-PLE.

The same principle goes for *sight-memory* too. It is a process that you can train your child's brain to work on: one, by focussing on tiny details to peg each into the brain; two, by giving every important detail equal attention to store the full picture.

Brain Train

There is no mystique involved in training your child's brain to remember efficiently. There are two extremely effective ways of developing your child's microfilm memory:

- The recalling method
- The sight method

The Recalling Method

According to Professor John Yuille of the University of British Columbia in Vancouver, who has carried out extensive research on this subject: 'The best way to remember something is to recall the information almost immediately. By storing away facts and then rapidly retrieving them, you open up more efficient pathways in the mind.'

When your child says 'Con-stan-ti-no-ple', make him recall it immediately. However, he obviously cannot walk around gabbling what he has just learnt! This is where a personal diary comes in handy.

Every evening, let him record the events of the day. Homework, in itself, is like a diary. If you feel he is already burdened with homework, you can discuss his dilemma with him and encourage him to *teach* you. For example, ask him, 'What did you learn in Maths today?'

148

Gently prod him to be more specific. 'HCF? What is that? It sounds really interesting! Can you show me how it is done?' Let him sit with you and explain it to you by working it out. The next day, he may tell his friends, 'My Mum is real dumb! She didn't know what HCF was!' But that will be a small price to pay!

I know one parent who makes her daughter jot down notes about other subjects too. For example, she will say, 'What did they teach you in Geography today?'

'About Greenland.'

'Greenland? How do you spell it? Write it down for me!' The child writes it down and shows it to her. Then she follows up with more questions that bring out answers like: It is the world's largest island. It has got an area of 2,175,600 square kilometres. It is in the Arctic Ocean....

By recalling what she has learnt, her daughter is unwittingly committing it to memory. Also, by writing it down, the child is able to organise the information. Every step and effort enhances the brain's power to retain facts, which Dr Yuille refers to so imaginatively as 'the pathways in the mind'.

The Sight Method

In Chapter 11, I have already written about how you can go about helping your child to develop a supermemory by discussing pictures from his favourite book. This way, you will provide him with what I call an *inner movie*.

This method is extremely important as it adds to the recall method. It strengthens your child's recalling ability. It adds muscle to it. For example, your child can actually *see* the alphabets of CONSTANTINOPLE. With both sound and sight working within his brain, his memory-bank is already being trained to operate efficiently.

Create Innovative Methods of Memorising

Former students of Bombay Scottish High School recall their History teacher, a Mr Krishnan, with great affection and respect. He introduced an innovative and interesting method that enhanced their ability to remember dates.

On the blackboard, he sketched out a winding path, with his characteristic quick movements. It was narrow at the top and wound its way to the bottom, getting broader and broader at the base. It gave the impression to the students that a path had started miles away, growing broader as it reached them. Then he drew lines — like horizontal stripes — inside the path. On each line, he wrote important dates in their chronological order. And against each date, he wrote the event. Every student drew this winding path in his notebook. Of course, initially, there was much giggling and nudging! But soon, the students settled down happily to their lessons as they realized that remembering dates had turned into a pleasure trip!

What Mr Krishnan did was not only to give a fresh and fun element to remembering dates, but he cleverly used the visual aspect too. For example, a date like 1857 would be visualised by the student as being at the head of the path. The event next to it — India's first attempt at independence — followed naturally. It made it so much easier to remember.

Why was Mr. Krishnan's path of dates so effective?

- Students could remember facts when they were presented in an organized chronological manner.

- The path helped link the date with an event visually. During exams, students could remember where the date was on the path. The event that was written next to the date then came to mind easily.

- The path also helped the students to remember which event came before or after the other. Thus, events could be linked in a logical pattern.

- The path saved the student from sitting over a dry list of dates and trying to memorise them. The imaginative and effective way of presenting dates motivated them into learning.

- The path was a ready reference, illustrating dates at a glance. It made the learning process effortless, and, therefore, easy.

- By drawing the path each time, the student taught himself. Research has shown that the best way to learn is to teach. Sounds strange? But it is true!

Krishnan's Path of Knowledge

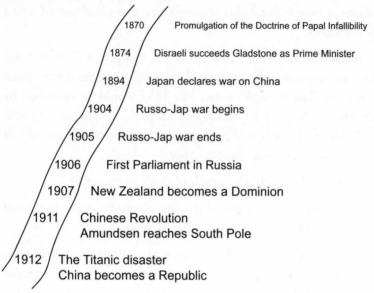

1870 — Promulgation of the Doctrine of Papal Infallibility

1874 — Disraeli succeeds Gladstone as Prime Minister

1894 — Japan declares war on China

1904 — Russo-Jap war begins

1905 — Russo-Jap war ends

1906 — First Parliament in Russia

1907 — New Zealand becomes a Dominion

1911 — Chinese Revolution
Amundsen reaches South Pole

1912 — The Titanic disaster
China becomes a Republic

Mr Krishnan's path of knowledge can be used by you for all subjects. It is an excellent method. It organises information in a logical manner. It helps the brain to peg on to each topic and absorb facts effectively and easily.

To Conclude

As I have said earlier, your child already has a microfilm memory. By implementing the two techniques I have discussed in this chapter, you can help him to develop it to its fullest potential.

A supermemory is a child's best friend. Developing a supermemory is a skill, which, when used, adds to super-understanding and superlearning. It is a vital link between all the other abilities that are required to turn your child into a genius.

17

Guideposts for the Genius

Genius does not argue; it creates.

Rabindranath Tagore

A genius is like a fountain. The water of knowledge surges through — recycling, regenerating, rejoicing in a burst of vibrant colours. But even the fountain gushes out its energy through guideposts set by the architect and operates on the natural laws of pressure. Similarly, even the most motivated genius needs guideposts to fuel his fountain of knowledge into higher realms, to add brilliance to those prisms of colours.

Setting up the Plinth

You can be the architect. You can set up the plinth and the guideposts, then step back, and let the child flower under his own natural pressure. As he gets into the mainstream, do not let any undercurrents like stress or anxiety tug him downwards.

This is where your role, as a parent, is supremely important. You have to give him the base, the most fundamental one being the management of time.

Time Management

You have provided your child with a well-lit, comfortable, cosy den. He has his own desk, chair and stationery. Now see to it that he sets aside a time for studying. It should never feel like a chore. Eating, drinking, playing, watching television, listening to music and other interesting activities are all a part of his life. So are studies. Obviously he or she must feel that studies are fun too.

To inculcate this positive attitude in him, first observe how he spends his time. Ask him to keep a record or log for a few days. Every half an hour, let him write down what he did. He is sure to be surprised to discover from his own record how much time he has been wasting.

During a particularly busy season, an exporter of garments found that he was literally tearing his hair out due to the work pressure. 'It got to a point where I found I was neglecting key areas,' he told me. He had to meet new suppliers, arrange

appointments with buyers, approve of designs, suggest new ones, go on inspections of finished consignments....

With every activity tugging at him in all directions, he finally locked himself up in his cabin and poured himself a cup of tea. Sipping the hot, refreshing beverage, he calmed down. In this peaceful state of mind, he pulled a pad and pen towards himself. Then he wrote down all the things he had to do.

'When I looked at the list,' he told me, 'I was surprised that despite all that hectic activity, I hadn't finished a single thing I had set out to do in the morning!' With a clear mind, he chalked out his schedule for the day. By evening, he had finished every item on his list to his immense satisfaction. After that day, he keeps his schedule on the desk in front of him, pencilling in changes when circumstances demand it.

Your child is not very different from this exporter. He has his school, his homework, his play, his hobbies, his studies to attend to. He needs a schedule to help him make better use of his time. And just like the exporter, he needs it to be flexible enough to allow shifts or changes whenever required.

Flexibility is very important because in no way should your child feel that he is missing out on the fun of life. Start by making him help you draw up a weekly schedule for him. It should include time for studying, relaxing, playing with his friends....

If your child has a Maths test on Thursday, and wants to go to a party on Wednesday night, what would you do?

Usually, you would reprimand him and remind him about his test. 'You can't go,' you would tell him. Sulkily, he would sit at his desk, simmering with resentment. He, probably, would not be able to concentrate on his studies and would fare badly in the test. You would feel vindicated! 'See! You wanted to go for that silly party. If you had gone, you would have probably failed!'

If you reacted in the manner as given above, what would happen? Your child would have missed out on the fun, and would score low marks. This would add insult to his injury. He would start disliking maths and his attitude would be set into a negative mould.

On the other hand, you could take a more positive approach. You and he could work out a weekly schedule. You could tell him, 'You have a Maths test on Thursday. So why don't you put in a little extra work on Monday and on Tuesday? That will leave you free for your Wednesday night party!' This way, you will be his friend, his accomplice. It is likely that he will willingly put in that little extra work, attend the Wednesday-night party and do well in his test on Thursday.

Do you see the difference? All it requires is a little bit of planning. Sometimes you may receive an unexpected invitation. Even so, if you already have a weekly schedule, all you have to do is adjust it around a bit. For example, your child can tidy up his room the following day. Here, your flexible attitude will come in handy. Sometimes it may even involve missing his favourite TV programme. But he will accept it happily if he realizes that you want him to have as much fun as he can in the long run.

By managing his time, you will set a broad, flexible plinth. Now you can put in the guideposts.

Reaching Your Goal

In Chapter 15 (Fostering Superlearning) I have touched briefly on the importance of finding out the main point of a given area of study. But it is no good telling your child, 'Read this and find out the main point of the subject.' You may as well be talking to him in Greek! It will be like locating a friend's new home in a strange area without any directions or landmarks! Directions stem from a known place, a known context.

If a friend tells you, 'You know where the Taj Mahal Hotel is? Well, drive straight down that road, take a left turn....' His directions are based on a place that you are already familiar with — a context.

Provide Directions

A good text book provides directions or guidelines to help students find their way through the subject matter. Look for the guidelines in the introduction, headings and summaries. Your child should first read these guidelines. They will give him a broad idea of what he is about to read. By reading the main body of the chapter, he will fill in the outline he has already formed in his mind. Then he should read the summary once again. The second reading will fix the main point in his mind. Never allow your child to make the mistake of concentrating on everything instead of trying to focus on the main idea.

A friend of mine was appearing for her final examination in Home Science in Nirmala Niketan, a reputed college in Bombay. For days and nights, she studied hard, but as the exam time approached, she told her father tearfully, 'I won't be able to appear for my exams. I can't remember anything!' Her father, a mechanical engineer by profession, was a brilliant man in his field of work. He did not have an inkling about her subjects. He did not even know how to brew tea! But he was a wise man, a practical man.

Quietly, he reassured her. Arming himself with her text books, he read every one of them. As he read, he made notes. He summarized each chapter, focussing on the main point. At the end of it, he handed his notes to her.

'Read them,' he advised calmly.

She did. Then she turned to her text books. She appeared for her exams with more confidence than she had ever done before. She not only passed with flying colours but came first in her class!

With her brilliant results, the college even selected her to be sent to Paris for an orientation programme!

'I don't know how my father did it!' she told me dazedly. To her it was an unbelievable experience — an engineer teaching Home Science! But what had her father actually done? He had focussed on the main idea of each chapter. In doing so, he had handed her the key to unlock the matter in each topic. He had also categorised the information into neat sections and given her a blueprint to work on — a blueprint which was clear and concise. Once she had grasped it, all that she had read began to make sense and she remembered everything!

Categorising is an important follow-up process to finding the main idea. For example, in a Science class, your child can learn about the varied species in the animal kingdom through categorising or grouping them into reptiles, mammals, fish, birds, amphibians.... Creating these smaller groups will help your child to absorb new information quickly and effectively. The trick here is that you are feeding the child's brain with smaller morsels of information. He will bite into every morsel, savour it and digest it. Whereas, if you were to push down a huge chunky piece, he would gag on it!

Groups can be created in different ways for different subjects. For example, if your child is studying about World War I in History, he can group events by geographic location, by a timeline (dates) or by specific countries involved.

If he is studying a foreign language, he can divide the words into nouns, pronouns, adjectives, adverbs, verbs, and so on.

Enhance Thinking Power

Thinking power can be enhanced through inter-related processes. After the child has read the summary, he should read the entire chapter. While doing so, he should fit the details into the appropriate places of the main outline as given in the summary. He should not consider the material as a list of unrelated facts. In other words, he should try to organize the information to form a complete picture. At the same time, he should also forge relationships or links between new information and his own previous knowledge and experience.

I have already touched on the key factors involved in this process in previous chapters. However, I will summarise them once again. In brief, help your child to focus his attention. Use auto-suggestion, build positive images and encourage questions.

To handle this superlearning strategy effectively, make him pause before each section. Check out if he has pinpointed the main idea, if he can create analogies and link ideas.

You need not stick rigidly to this format. Sometimes a topic may have two main points. The child can pause at this stage and discuss them with you. This will show that his mental powers are broadening and that he is thinking independently for himself. Encourage him in this process. He can try several different approaches and decide for himself which method works best for which subject.

To Conclude

So far, you have created the structure and set up the guideposts for the fountain of knowledge. If this plinth is functioning efficiently as a firm base, if it is bubbling, rising, billowing ... your child is ready to create and build his own guideposts. To find out what they are, turn the page, and read on...!

18

Imprints of a Genius

Train up a child in the way he should go; and when he is old, he will not depart from it.

New Testament

I was being shown around a school by the principal. As we walked down the long corridors, I glanced into the classrooms. Rows of uniformed students were bent over their books, writing notes. I cannot explain why, but I felt suffocated. How I wished I could gather every child in the world and give him or her the basic necessities — food, shelter, clothes, love and education. The principal seemed to sense my mood and share it.

Later, over a cup of tea, she said quietly, 'You felt it too, didn't you?' At my nod, she continued, 'I don't know what I've enjoyed more — being a student or a principal.'

'Do you personally keep a track of every student?' I asked curiously. She sighed.

'I wish I could. But I question my teachers about the performance of students in their respective subjects. And I try to keep little jottings about each student — his or her strengths and weaknesses. Then I meet the parents to try and make them understand how they can help their children.'

'What have you learned from this exercise?' I asked.

'Several things,' she replied. 'Curiously, I find that except for emotional upsets in the child's personal life which need specialised attention, most other situations have one remedy.'

'And that is?'

She looked at me almost apologetically. 'It's like saying one tablet can cure varied ills. But I find, that if the student is encouraged to take notes on his own, he understands almost anything.'

'Is it so simple?' I asked.

She smiled. 'Most remedies in life are simple.'

Her words have always remained with me. Your child may be a superlearner and have a supermemory. But even a genius cannot remember everything he reads. In fact, a genius will soon realise that it is not necessary to try to remember everything.

Summarise in Your Own Words

How should a child go about remembering matter?

First, he should sift and select the most important information. Then he should make notes of the main points. These notes will serve as a summary of the most important points. Note-making will automatically make him review the subject. He will categorise the material, understand it and, of course, remember it. It is a simple, yet extremely effective exercise.

However, your child should be made to understand that note-taking is different from copying. If he blindly copies what he reads, it will be an exercise in futility. He should understand the matter and write it down in his own words. For example, suppose he reads this sentence:

Tucked away in a corner of the Yucatan peninusla between Mexico and Guatemala, the tiny country known today as Belize was a major centre of Mayan civilization for more than 600 years.

If he copies it down word for word, he may not understand the meaning. What he could do is break it up and write:

Belize is a tiny country. It is in a corner of the Yucatan peninsula. It is situated between Mexico and Guatemala. Once upon a time, Belize was inhabited by the Mayan civilization. The Mayan lived in Belize for more than 600 years.

It is imperative that he learns how to interpret what he reads and makes notes at home. Note-making, while reading, will make him understand and grasp what he reads. But it will also give him practice and prepare him for taking notes in the classroom, which is more challenging. While reading, he can always refer to the book again. But it is nearly impossible to re-hear a lecture or class discussion. He may take a tape recorder to class if the teacher allows it. But students who have tried this have found it ineffective. It only doubles their work. If the lecture was for one hour, they have to spend the same amount of time listening to the tape. Then they have to make notes. It is a time-consuming job and not always effective or efficient.

Classroom Notes

When the teacher talks fluently and at length about a subject, the child may feel: How can I take down every thing? I'm not a tape recorder! The solution is: Do not take down everything. Train your child to look out for clues on what is important.

- If a teacher writes on the blackboard, it is worth taking notes. Teachers use this practice to emphasise points.

- If the teacher spends a lot of time on one subject, the information must be taken down.

- Listen closely to the teacher's voice. Her voice will indicate what is important. For example, she may slow down and talk in deliberate tones. This is because she wishes to state

something clearly and precisely, and it is important and must be taken down.

- The teacher may repeat certain important points so that if the child missed them the first time, he will get another opportunity to jot them down.

- The teacher's phrases hold vital clues. Teachers use such phrases like 'three reasons for ...' or 'the purpose of ...' or 'the main point here ...' or 'in summary....' Such phrases are pointers that what she is about to say is important. Sometimes, she pauses before she goes on, to make the child realize that what she has just said is important and that he should write it down.

You can even hold a mock practice session at home to prepare your child for the real thing.

Book Markings

Your child should look out for words or sentences written in capital letters, bold typeface or italics. These are indicators of important points.

Train your child never to skip diagrams and tables. Combined with the written word, they are extremely effective aids and facilitate a better understanding.

There is an equally effective alternative to note-making. But it can be done only if the text book belongs to your child and is not borrowed from the school library or a friend. Since it involves marking the book, ownership is a must.

Here is how your child can mark the book:

Horizontal underlining/highlight pen — This method can be used to indicate the main idea. Here, highlighting makes more sense. Visually, it is more pleasing and the words stand out boldly in front of your child's eye.

Vertical lines — A vertical line can be used in the margin if the main idea is contained in more than one line or sentence.

Asterisks — This can be used to indicate links between information on two pages. For example, if there is something about a turtle on page 1 and again on page 3, put an asterisk in the margin. Next to it, write: see page 3, or see page 1.

Numbers — Place within the text, numbers such as 1, 2, 3... to indicate a series or list of points to be remembered.

Word formations — If your child wants to remember several points in a topic, he can take the first alphabet of every important word and form a word. For example, if he wants to remember the various parts of the eye: cornea, upper eyelid, retina, lens — he can form the word *Curl*. He can enter this word in the margin this way:

Cornea

Upper eyelid

Retina

Lens

This will provide him with a quick and easy reference and instant recall of the parts of the eye.

Circles or boxes — Place these around new words to be learned.

Notes in the margin — Your child's own ideas that spring up from this information can be noted down in the margin. Do not let him write summaries here because it will only make the page messy. And he may not even feel like looking at it again! But fresh ideas will add to his thinking power.

Loose-Leaf notebook paper — Many parents tend to buy notebooks for their children, but such books are limiting since the pages are bound together permanently. It is, therefore, advisable to buy large 8½ x 11 inch sheets of loose-leaf notebook paper. This size will allow your child to include diagrams next to the written notes. Buy him a file so that the sheets can be placed together. This method is effective because he can add more information from other sources in an orderly manner. A bound note book does not give him this flexibility.

Preparing the pages — Before the child starts writing down notes, he should prepare the pages. He should draw a vertical line, approximately two inches from the left edge of each sheet. This can be his extra information or summarising margin. He can also use this space later for key words, phrases, sub-headings or new ideas. During class or while reading, he should write only on the right hand and broader side of the page.

The left-hand column can be used to jot down sub-headings. For example, if the child has written notes on the American Revolution, he can later jot down broad sub-headings such as:

165

Causes, Declaration of Independence, Major battles, and so on. This will serve as a quick and easy reference.

Use Paragraphs — As the child writes, he should train himself to use separate paragraphs. He can figure out when it is time for a new paragraph from the teacher's attitude. For example, when the teacher says, 'Now, we will take up ...' or 'Let's turn to page ...' such phrases are keys to a new paragraph.

Phrases and Abbreviations — Due to the speed of talking while teaching, your child can jot down phrases rather than try to write the entire sentence. He can also use abbreviations, provided he can, later, figure out what they stand for. For example, if the teacher says:

'When the South American colony of Dutch Guiana became the independent Republic of Surinam in 1975, it suffered an immediate economic setback...,'

Your child can write:

'S. Amer. col of Dutch Guiana became ind. rep of Surinam-1975-imme eco setback.'

He need not use numbers for paragraphs since it is time-consuming and he could miss out what the teacher has to say.

To Conclude

Note-taking is an exciting adventure for your child. The methods suggested in this chapter are simple, yet effective. If a child has older brothers and sisters, he can pick up note-making tips from them too. Note-making is a creative effort. It facilitates clarity and organisation. The genius and his notes are, indeed, an awesome combination!

19

Chronicle of a Genius

Inspiration and genius — one and the same.

Victor Hugo

Your child's notes are like a chronicle of his genius. With knitted eyebrows and his tongue sticking out endearingly, he reads, listens, interprets and jots down with great concentration and effort. If you put his note files away after he has no further use for them, years later — when you find them in an old trunk in your attic — you will be able to trace the growth of his genius. There will be little indicators: a childish scrawl turning into an adult flow, faulty spellings, awkward language and such pointers. What a delightful rediscovery it will be!

Self-Assessment Through Notes

Meanwhile, as a responsible parent, you owe it to your child to make sure that his notes are useful to him. They should be a source of knowledge as well as enjoyment. In fact they should serve as a measure of self-assessment or self-testing. Seeing his file grow under his eyes, and filled with increasing knowledge, will give the child a great lift!

However, along with quantity of information, you should ensure that there is quality too. Your child should realise the value of his notes by respecting them. They are the rungs on the ladder of his success. Only if he applies them to learning, will he proceed ahead.

The reason I am stressing this point is the appalling way I have seen note-taking and notes being regarded and handled. Many students tend to copy from their friends. Sometimes, parents assist or encourage to copy. No attempt is made to understand what is being written down. Prior to a test or an examination, the student pulls out the notes, memorises them and goes off to the examination hall to do his paper.

This is a waste of time and education. If the child has been ill and needs to copy notes from others due to lack of time, even then, he or she should make an attempt to understand what he is writing

down. Unfortunately, many parents view the child's education only as a means of getting the final degree — that printed piece of scroll which opens doors to his future career. What they miss out on understanding is that the child has not extracted the valuable treasure of education in the learning process. A child who has been taught independence and superlearning skills adds a definite plus to his degree. There is, indeed, a world of difference between a learner and a superlearner.

How to Use Notes

How should the superlearner use his notes? If he does not follow a systematic method, his notes will serve no purpose at all.

Review Immediately

Notes should be read as soon as possible — preferably, after that particular class during which he wrote them down. If that is not possible, he should spend about half an hour after school, perusing them. This way, he can complete or write out more clearly, any incomplete or confusing notes. He can do this exercise efficiently because the information is still fresh in his mind.

For example, let us say that the child has jotted down the following sentences:

Use of the port.lang in Br, Angola &

Moz pt to the early power of Port....

If he reviews his notes the same day, he will recapitulate that he has written about the Portuguese language in Brazil. On the other hand, if he were to read the notes a month or so later, he may wonder if the Br refers to Britain or, perhaps, Barbados! Immediate reviewing adds to efficient superlearning because it ensures immediate recall and accuracy.

Self-Testing

Self-testing is a powerful aid for a potential genius. He should test himself to see what he knows and does not know. Some facts tend to stick and stay easily in the memory. But some tend to get overlooked and forgotten. Self-testing ensures that a child never forgets any important point. It will make him use his study time more efficiently because he can then apply himself to reading and remembering what he had overlooked.

Let us take an example: your child is learning about China. The chapter on China deals with many aspects of the country. It devotes paragraphs to its major cities, its agricultural products, population, religions, leaders and its political system.

Your child has taken down notes. Now, he should look at the sub-headings in the left-hand side margin and question himself:

Q. What is the capital of China?

A. Beijing.

Q. What form of government does China have?

A. It is a communist republic.

Q. When was the Great Wall built?

A. In the third century B.C.

Supertesting

The above questions are simple and straightforward, requiring factual answers. But your child needs this foundation for more searching questions which you should supply him with for an effective self-evaluation.

For example:

Q. Why does China place so much emphasis on growing food?

Q. Why was the Great Wall built?

Q. How does the government affect the lives of the Chinese people?

By asking such questions, your child will add the new information to his previous fund of knowledge. He will then analyse the matter and be able to come up with intelligent answers. This ability to superunderstand will help him to assimilate any new information in an informed, educated manner. In short, his analytical skills or thinking power will be sharpened.

The Best Self-Testing Exercise

The best way to test himself is for your child to cover the right-hand side of the page and make up questions from the phrases and sub-headings in the left-hand column. He should answer each of the questions and then check the answers for accuracy by reading through the corresponding notes. This will help him to decide which sections need re-reading for better remembering.

From Chapter 17 onwards, I have detailed how you can create an infrastructure for studying: the guideposts you can supply the child with, how the genius should make his notes, and finally, how he should use and apply them.

At first, this may appear like an enormous task. You may feel it requires too much time in terms of planning or rescheduling. But any new method, by its very newness, appears difficult at first. Once you get into it, it will become a habit with you and your child. You will then find that your child takes less time to study but absorbs more efficiently.

The I.Q. Syndrome

Ever as you scan this headline, I can see your mind working. Your first thought will be: 'Genius has to have a high I.Q.' You will be surprised if I tell you that you are not entirely right. Let me put it this way — you cannot just fill the child with a vast amount of knowledge, and expect him to go for an I.Q. test and come out with flying colours. He may be the most knowledgeable child in the room where the test is conducted. But have you also given him love, confidence and a good self-image for him to be able to rise to the occasion? These factors are as important as knowledge.

What is I.Q.? It stands for Intelligence Quotient. An I.Q. test shows the relationship between the child's mental growth and development, and his age. An I.Q. score of 90-110 is considered to be normal or average. A score of above 130 is considered above average. A score of above 140 is that of a genius.

But while it is fine to subject your child to an I.Q. test, I am more concerned about your reaction after you know the score. If your child scores above 140, I foresee no problems. You will embrace your child and be happy. What concerns me is that, if by chance, your child scores below the genius-level, you will be unhappy. You will feel that all your inputs have been wasted. You will want to stop giving your child the kind of attention you have given earlier. You will slacken in your efforts. If you do this, you will be wrong, so wrong!

It is possible that at the time of giving the test, your child was not well or was over-anxious. In any case, I think it is wise not to place too much importance on the score. It is also possible that some of the questions were beyond his experiences. So, never change your attitude or lessen your efforts. While I am not undermining the I.Q. test potential, what I am emphasising on is your reaction to it. If you use the methods in this book, your child should definitely score over 140. If he does not, there could be extraneous circumstances that are genuinely beyond his control. But never taunt him about a low score. You will only undermine his intelligence. You will destroy the self-image he has. In fact, ask yourself where you have gone wrong. Re-read certain chapters in this book and strengthen your weak areas vis-a-vis your child.

To Conclude

Encourage and teach your child how to make useful notes that will help him to assimilate the information into his brain's storehouse of knowledge. Let him understand how to measure his level of learning and set a high standard for himself. Never, never have a negative attitude towards your child. A genius only blossoms in positive circumstances. Give your child all you've got — it's worth it!

20

Sustaining a Genius

The man who wins is the man who thinks he can.

Anon

I am assuming that since you have reached the final chapter of the book, you have already set your child on the great, glorious, sunshine-filled path towards becoming a genius; that you have worked towards liberating the tremendous creative powers within him or her; that you have focussed and set goals, and turned your child into a superlearner.

If you have, you will find that the various processes involved have also made him a hard worker. Since he is gripped by the interesting and fascinating world of knowledge, since his intellectual buds have been tickled, he will want to explore more and delve further.

You have played a key role in your child's development so far. You must have realized that with each new step, each new stage, the support and help you had to provide was different. Now that your child is a regular school-goer, you will also have to monitor his progress.

Some parents feel that once their child has entered the great portals of school, their own responsibility ends. They feel that the rest is up to the teachers. Not at all! The parent always remains the primary source of knowledge, love, security and care for the child. So it is only a natural progression that you meet his teacher as often as is possible. Some schools have specific days when parents can meet teachers. At such times, parents should seize the opportunity to establish a friendly link with the teachers, and convey to them that they would like to cooperate in any way they can.

When parents and teachers have a good rapport, the child gains. The teacher gets to know the child as a student and as a member of a team, and can keep the parent informed on these developments. The latter can, in turn, provide information about the child's character and potential.

Many parents hesitate to go to their child's school. Their hesitation stems from a genuine feeling that the teacher may think that they are interfering. There is also the fear that their questions may be misunderstood as criticism. Teachers, however, are not the strict, stern dragons they are made out to be. They are human too! They too want the best for the children they teach. What the parents should do is to try and establish a rapport with the teacher from the very first day of school itself. Later, when they find that their child is particularly enthusiastic about a certain subject due to the teacher's excellent attitude and methods, they can send her a warm note of appreciation by mail. Such thoughtful actions encourage the teacher and set the stage for a cooperative relationship.

How to Handle a Problem at School

The parent-teacher link is extremely vital. If parents establish links with the teacher from the beginning, they will have an open communication. If they don't, and their child is unhappy, restless or fidgety, they will meet the teacher for the first time only when confronted with a problem. Had links been established earlier, it would be so much simpler to communicate with the teacher.

175

Let me suggest what you should do in such a situation. If your child comes home looking depressed or crying, do not be upset. You must remain calm to calm him down. If he manages to convey to you what he feels has gone wrong, do not ring up the teacher immediately. Such thoughtless, impulsive actions help nobody. If your attitude is positive, it will reach out to the teacher, who, in turn, will want to help your child. Who gains? Your child, of course!

For the best results, you could consider these steps:

- Calm down. Think and decide what questions you would like to ask the teacher. Write them down.
- Ring up the teacher and cordially request for a short meeting. Your tone should be friendly and cooperative.
- When you meet the teacher, don't start shouting all at once. It will sound like you are criticising the teacher. Explain quietly what is troubling you. The teacher may have some information that you were unaware of. Once you know it, you will be glad that you did not take a confrontationist attitude. Now both of you can work towards easing the problem for your child.
- On your part, answer the teacher's questions frankly and as completely as you can. The more insight you provide, the more effective she can be in dealing with the problem.
- Seek out the teacher's expectations for classroom behaviour, homework and parental involvement. Ask the teacher to suggest steps you can take at home.
- Follow the teacher's recommendations. Based on her experience, she may be able to give you some tips on additional home-learning activities.

Let us take an illustrative case: Everything came easy to this little girl who was a genius. So much so that her mother sensed that she was getting complacent, even slipshod or casual about her lessons. She did not like the child's increasingly patronizing attitude towards everything.

'What should I do?' she asked the teacher.

'She needs something more difficult to put her teeth into,' the teacher advised. She needs to be challenged.

After much thought and discussion, they worked out a programme. The little girl was enrolled into a computer class. She did well there too. But there was a difference. She found that she had to make more of an effort. Her patronizing attitude vanished. The balance was restored.

Accept the Challenge

I have lived by an axiom that has helped me all my life: Every day, every thing I do is a new beginning. There is no end to possibilities or opportunities. You must induct this belief into yourself and your child.

You must believe that there is an eternal well-spring of power within you and your child. A well-spring that you can tap to release the genius in your child.

If you want to enhance the great intelligence, the marvellous gift in your child there are several things that you must do:

Sow the seeds of genius — This is no metaphorical myth. You can do it if you believe that you can.

Pour in your creative inputs — It is your creative inputs, your efforts that will help your child to flower into a genius.

Create a superhome — Make your home a happy shrine for education.

Narrate bedtime stories. Wise thoughts and attitudes are often embedded in such tales. Use this method often.

Make your child read, write and think — *By* doing this, you are opening the doors of knowledge for your tiny traveller in his journey of life.

Make his life a playground — *To* a child, everything is fun. The innocent mind is always open to learning. Let him learn with fun.

Bring out the achiever in him — *You* can do this by giving him a strong self-image. Encourage him; never discourage him.

Propel him with motivation — Bring out his inner power and potential by motivating him.

Instil in him the secrets of superlearning — Lead him to this great land. With superunderstanding and a supermemory he will be ready for the glorious life of a superachiever.

Set guidelines for him — In the land of superlearning, set these important channels and markers so that he can be knowledgeable, a wealthy individual and a genius.

Bear in mind the famous saying: A winner never quits; a quitter never wins. I believe that the legendary cricketer, the little master — Sunil Gavaskar — keeps this reminder on his table. It goes for you too. Life is there to be taken head-on. You can motivate your child if you adopt the three P's: *Perseverance, Patience and a Positive attitude.*

To conclude — *You* can turn your child into a genius! You can if you have read this book, live by it and learn from it. You can do it if you believe in the four inspiring words, the magic *mantras* of motivation:

I CAN DO IT!

And with this glorious *mantra,* you will enjoy the fruits of your efforts when you can sit back, and smile and say:

MY CHILD IS A GENIUS!

Personal Notes